MICHAEL PHELPS

MICHAEL PHELPS:
The Untold Story of a Champion

Bob Schaller

Introduction by Rowdy Gaines
Foreword by Jason Lezak

St. Martin's Griffin ☒ New York

www.stmartins.com

ISBN-10: 0-312-57381-2
ISBN-13: 978-0-312-57381-2

First Edition: October 2008

10   9   8   7   6   5   4   3   2   1

To the relay members of the 2008 U.S. Men's Olympic team, and all the men and women on the 2008 U.S. swimming team, for showing character in and out of the pool we can all be proud of—and an extended appreciation to Michael Phelps for being both superhuman, and very human.

Contents

Foreword
By Jason Lezak, 2008 U.S. Olympic relay double-gold medal anchor, 100 freestyle bronze medalist

I have been a teammate of Michael Phelps since the 2000 Sydney Olympics in Australia. To see him grow as an athlete and a person through the years has been something I have enjoyed.

I really did think eight gold medals were possible for Michael. I knew there would be some tough races. I expected that 100 fly to be the close race that it was. Some said it was lucky, but the fact is that he won, and he was willing to do whatever it took to push himself to win that race that day, to claim that moment and gold medal. The irony is, no one realizes that even if he had "lost" that race, seven golds and one silver would still have been the best Olympic performance in the history of the Games.

What Michael did is a great accomplishment. Our entire team did a lot of good things, and a lot of us stepped up to a new level and achieved our own dreams. Aaron Peirsol had a pair of golds and silver. Brendan Hansen finished strong to help us get medley-relay gold. Ian Crocker finished with a gold. Ryan Lochte had a great Games. I had some Olympic disappointments that had me thinking about retiring after the 2004 Olympics. I am so glad I did not retire. I still felt like there was something missing. After what we did in Beijing, I feel like I accomplished something I set out to do four years ago. That does not mean I am going to retire now, because I love the sport and I love what I am doing.

The 2008 Olympics were memorable for a lot of us, and I hope all of you. I had two big goals in 2008 for Beijing. My first was getting back to winning the individual medal that I thought I would win in the 100 freestyle at the 2004 Games where I had gone out too slow in the preliminaries, and did not make the final. My other goal was to help get the U.S. back on track by winning the 400 freestyle relay. We wanted to re-establish and show our dominance in that event.

We had another event to re-establish ourselves in as a relay power, the 400 medley relay. At the 2007 World Championships in Melbourne, Australia, we missed the opportunity to swim in the final because of a disqualification in the preliminary. No one was putting the blame on anybody else. But still, we wanted to go out and show the world we could dominate.

The rest of the world is catching up to us in a lot

of events. That is a good thing for swimming, because it shows a lot more young people are swimming around the world than ever before, and are choosing swimming as both a competitive sport and lifestyle. But it also meant in 2008 that we would have to get better.

At the 2008 Games, we certainly did not have the same dominance as we did in 2004, because back then we were three seconds ahead of everybody in the 400 medley relay. However, the Olympics are about doing your best and winning. We knew this time it would not be a cakewalk, and that several other nations would be contenders for the gold medals, and that other countries with a good chance to medal could step it up and do the best relay they've ever done and perhaps take a gold medal.

But we were golden in all three relays. And yes, that last leg of the 400 free relay was as hard as it looked for me—anchoring the medley relay was also a challenge where we met the challenge, and I'm very proud to be a part of that team. It wasn't easy, but when something is worthwhile, it usually takes your best effort. That's what we did.

Preface:
Let the Games Begin: China, 2008

At 8:08 p.m. local time on August 8, 2008, the attention of the world focused on Beijing, China.

The biggest, most populous country and burgeoning superpower cracked open its doors to the rest of the world. China largely kept its doings concealed behind the Great Wall, only allowing the outside world the occasional well-orchestrated glimpse, often through conflict about freedoms in Tibet, and even Hong Kong. Tiananmen's Square in Beijing was about to be transformed from political and historical chess piece into a tourism landmark. It became the public gathering place that most would visit on the way to the Water Cube and the Bird's Nest, hosts to swimming and track, respectively, at the 2008 Summer Olympic Games.

As the curtain was drawn to unveil the Forbidden City to the world, the world knew only about its most recent, most temporary import: American swimmer, Michael Phelps. His Olympic quest was its own form of dynasty, one that started internationally with the 2000 Games. As the surprise second qualifier in the 200 butterfly, after top-ranked veteran, Tom Malchow, Phelps was a gangly 15-year-old on his way to the continent where swimming is king: Australia. Down under, swimming superstars make the millions that athletes like LeBron James or Peyton Manning might in the United States.

A few months after those 2000 Olympics in Sydney, I sat down with Michael Phelps for what would be the first of several yearly interviews to talk about who he was, where he was headed, and how he would get there. His coach, Bob Bowman, was also along that day and with us for several of the other interviews that would follow in the years to come.

The 2004 Olympics in Athens, Greece, were tentatively planned as the place for Phelps' coronation. He had a slim chance to equal Mark Spitz's record of seven medals, and no chance of getting eight. One of the events he was swimming was new to him; he even admitted he just wanted to swim that particular race for the experience. The world record holder, Ian Thorpe, was competing and among the five or six better than Phelps in that race.

Fast-forward four years: Everybody in swimming, and many outside of it, had an opinion on what Michael Phelps could or could not do in China. Gary Hall Jr., the timeless, but never speechless, Olympic sprinter, said there was no way Phelps would get eight golds. He knew one specific race that Phelps would lose. Ian Thorpe pointed out that the new, never-before-done scheduling and times of the races would have Phelps so out of his routine that there was no way he could get gold in all the races.

The only voice aside from those standing behind Phelps logistically—coaches, teammates—who seemed to think Phelps had a chance was one who stood the most to lose if Phelps did pull off the feat: Mark Spitz. With a candor and humility that Spitz had only shown in recent years after being a bit reclusive with his iconic status and legendary haul of gold medals some thirty-six years earlier, Spitz showed up at the 2008 Olympic Trials in Omaha, Nebraska, and in the Heartland spilled open his own thoughts and feelings on Phelps and the record: He could and would do it, Spitz said.

On 8-08-08 at 8:08 p.m. in China, the Games began.

Acknowledgments

This book was edited by Michael's teammate from the 2000 Sydney Games, B.J. Bedford-Miller, who also swam with Michael's sister, Whitney. B.J., a published author herself, helped focus the story and explain its technical terms. My indebtedness to USA Swimming is well-documented—writing for them as a freelance Web and magazine contributor was invaluable in researching this book. All quotes not attributed were done by me interviewing these athletes and coaches, and other information was also gathered through USA Swimming, including quotes from the Beijing Games and press conference transcripts that were made available to all media. Thanks to the University of Michigan swimmers who provided context and breadth to the story; because of their character, I now know the integrity, candor, truthfulness, and pride it takes to be a "Michigan Man." This project was not possible without literary agent Bob Diforio's exhaustive promotion of, and belief in, this book. My appreciation is extended to Matthew Shear, Marc Resnick, and Sarah Lumnah at St. Martin's for shepherding this great story into publication—I'm grateful there are still a few publishers who care about doing important, meaningful books.

Introduction
by Rowdy Gaines, three-time
Olympic gold medalist and
NBC commentator

In one amazing week, he made history—history that may never again be repeated.

Michael Phelps is a name that has become synonymous not just with the sport of swimming, but with the highest level of perfection achieved in all of Olympic history. A total of eight gold medals in the 2008 Beijing Olympics is an awesome feat that will be nearly impossible to match. And added to his six golds in Athens, Michael has become the most prolific Olympic gold medalist in any sport.

Even with my more than twenty years of covering swimming, I wondered if it was possible for Michael to win all of his events in Beijing. After all, it would require almost twenty races and would depend on teamwork in three separate relay events. Now, I can say that it was my greatest honor and privilege to have broadcast all of Michael's races for

NBC at the 2008 Olympic Games in Beijing. Along with my partner Dan Hicks, I witnessed a performance that our sport and the Olympic movement may never see again, eight gold medals and seven world records. And it wasn't just the two of us; more people watched the 2008 Beijing Olympics than any in history, more than 214 million in the U.S. alone.

If you had asked a Hollywood scriptwriter to produce a screenplay for a motivational movie on swimming, he couldn't have created more drama than we saw: How does Michael swim the 200 butterfly with his goggles filled with water, literally swimming the final fifty meters completely blind and counting his strokes to the wall—and still break the world record while winning?

How does Michael win a race by 1/100th of a second, the very slimmest of margins in the sport of swimming—a race so close that it has to go to photographic proof to confirm his victory?

How does Michael inspire Jason Lezak, the thirty-two-year-old long-time sprint anchor, to finish the 400 free relay with his fastest split ever by more than a second?

How does he do it? Because his whole life has been history in the making. When Michael finished the 200 butterfly at his first Olympics in Sydney, the youngest U.S. male Olympian in sixty years, I saw in his eyes that there was so much more he wanted to accomplish. That very young man had a hunger like no one else I'd met, and I will never forget Michael telling me in Sydney that he had a purpose in life . . . to change the landscape of our sport forever.

Four years earlier in Athens, his six gold medals and two bronze showed that landscape changing, but it was only the beginning. Now I know what he meant in Sydney. What he has accomplished will change his life and swimming forever. Michael is doing for swimming what Tiger Woods has done for golf; he has generated immense interest in the sport with people around the world, many of them new enthusiasts. And among them are future Olympians who see him as the tremendous role model he will always be.

Part I

Chapter 1

Raised by a Single Mom and Two Amazing Sisters

While Michael Phelps was worrying about the things most nine-year-old boys do—what sports he should play, how come he had so much homework—the Phelps as a family had moved into a nice home in the Baltimore suburb of Harford County.

However, when his parents, Fred, a state trooper, and mother, Debbie, at the time a home economics teacher, divorced, the kids and their mother moved to a townhouse in Rodgers Forge, a middle-class suburb of Baltimore.

His oldest sister, Hilary, was only a couple years from heading off to college. The middle child, Whitney, was closer to Michael in age, so she spent a lot of time with her little brother, especially as their mother worried about running a household, building her own career—she was headed for a job in administration before becoming a middle-school principal—and taking care of getting her active kids to all their sporting events.

Michael's Attention Deficit Hyperactivity Disorder was, thanks to his mother, diagnosed at a young age.

"He was always full of energy. He'd talk constantly, and ask questions nonstop. He also had trouble focusing in school, and his teachers said they couldn't get him to interact during learning time. He was always pushing, nudging, shoving, and fidgeting. It was hard for him to listen unless it was something that really captivated his attention," Debbie Phelps told *Good Housekeeping* magazine. "Michael's doctor prescribed a stimulant medication. He only took it Monday through Friday, though—no weekends, no vacations, no holidays. I knew he'd benefit from the medication at school."

Whitney said she was aware of Michael's attention deficit condition.

"I know growing up when he was diagnosed, he was on medication," Whitney said. "He was a young boy that had tons of energy. I think our whole family might have a touch of it. I can't sit still and watch a movie, I can't just focus on one thing, and Michael was that way. I never really thought anything of it. A lot of kids have that."

The disorder, or illness, affected Michael mostly in school, though Whitney could see how it affected him at home when he had to sit for long periods, whether he was doing homework or even just watching a program on television, especially if he had little interest in it.

"Maybe it slowed him down in the classroom because sitting there, people with ADHD have a hard time sitting through a half-hour, forty-five-minute, or fifty-minute class," Whitney said. "Or even to watch a whole TV show from start to finish—it is hard to concentrate for that long. Once out of the school setting, though, sports really helped him because of the focus—he played lacrosse and baseball when he was younger, and when he'd do that or swimming it did not affect him."

Hilary said Michael was quite an athlete in every sport he attempted.

"Michael was awesome at playing all sports," Hilary said. "He was fast on his feet and had a lot of energy, so he could cover that lacrosse field like no other. Michael liked to win, so he always gave it his best. I think it would be hard to win every game if you played a team sport like baseball or lacrosse, but Michael still likes to win, and in the sport of swimming, he can give it his all, to make sure that he wins."

Michael agreed that it was a problem in school.

"I couldn't sit still, I couldn't focus," Michael told *The Sun* newspaper of London.

But he didn't appreciate it when, in middle

school, a teacher criticized him and told him his future was limited.

"One of my teachers at middle school—I can't remember his name—said I would never be successful," Michael told the *Sun*. "When someone says that, I'm going to work even harder to prove him wrong. It was a dream come true to achieve something no one has done before."

Debbie realized her son needed help focusing, and was not willing to let him use his ADHD as a crutch.

"Kids need structure. Kids need consistency," Debbie told The Associated Press. "I don't care if they have ADHD or not, they have to have those parameters in order to be successful."

His mother said she and Michael's sisters, along with swimming, helped him manage his condition.

"Our family became a team, and the girls paid attention to Michael's eating habits," Debbie said on Everyday Health's Web site. "We also observed time restrictions on some activities to teach him time management, and he began making choices so that he could use his time more wisely, just as he would at the pool. Michael has a mental toughness. He's very intense, but he never used to be able to focus. But even at ages nine and ten, at swim meets he would be focused for four hours—even though he'd only be swimming himself for three to four minutes—because swimming is his passion."

Hilary said their mom had not just the right career and education, but also the right temperament to help Michael deal with his ADHD.

"She has a lot of patience and worked really hard with all of us to instill solid values. I was away at college, but would hear about the things that she would do with Michael—help him with visualization exercises to help calm him if he was full of energy. She knew different ways to engage him in activities, as well as ways to help him focus."

Swimming was one of the keys in helping Michael deal with it.

"Getting in the water helped me focus and stay on track and I grew out of it," Michael said.

Whereas lacrosse and baseball are played on fields and are team sports, there is an occasional lull for certain players, especially in baseball.

"Swimming helped even more" with the ADHD, Whitney said, "because you have a pool that you stay inside, you can't run around all over the place, so it gave you certain boundaries and brought a certain focus."

Michael was also a victim of bullying, especially at school.

"There were days when I was on the school bus and had my baseball hat thrown out of the window," Michael told the *Sun*. "It's funny because the people who did that are now trying to come back and be friends, and it's like, 'No.'"

Debbie said the bullying developed a sense of

grounding in Michael that later helped him deal with fame.

"... Growing up, he had to deal with a lot of teasing and tormenting from other kids his age," his mother told *Good Housekeeping* magazine. "He was so tall and elongated that his hands were below his knees. He had a hard time going through that, but I think overcoming it helped him become the grounded person he is today."

Hilary said Michael did endure bullying, and that it was an eye-opener to the family that kids treated her brother that way.

"That was pretty tough," Hilary said. "Kids can be cruel and really mean. I think it's helped Michael take things with a grain of salt. When there are things written about him, he uses them for motivation. He's able to turn things that happen into a learning experience and grow from them."

While the bullying made school less enjoyable for Michael, he did like spending time with his sisters and their friends.

"There is a significant age difference with me and Michael, and when I was in high school, he was in elementary school," Hilary said. "Michael always wanted to be where the action was, which sometimes meant hanging out with me and my girlfriends. At the time, I wanted him to leave us alone, because he always had so much energy. But he's always been very thoughtful and kind."

Hilary was starting college at the University of Richmond at about the time Michael started to get national attention as a swimmer at age eleven. But Whitney said the time in the townhouse drew the close quartet even closer as a family.

"Hilary was in college, but when she would come home, we'd switch around, and decide who would be sleeping on the couch or who would be sleeping together," Whitney said. "I left for college—I went to UNLV—shortly after that. For a long time after that, it was just my brother and my mom. When we were all together at the house, it was crazy with all the different schedules. When we did all get together it was hilarious, because from all of us being swimmers and [with] training, we'd just get in a slap-happy mode, and we'd end up laughing on the floor."

Whitney said once her father left, the family used the experience to draw together even more.

"We have a very close family and love each other unconditionally," Whitney said. "No matter what, we can come back to the circle, we know that, and one of us will always be there for the other. That has shaped us into the people we are today."

One of the benefits for whomever Michael ends up marrying is that he knows how to act and behave around women after living with three of them.

"He definitely did go through training at a young age on how to be around girls, from the three of us," Whitney said.

Being closer in age to Michael left Whitney with a lot of time to spend with her relatively shy, although sometimes precocious, brother.

"Michael and I are five years apart, so we're a lot closer in age," Whitney said. "There's seven years between Michael and Hilary. Seven years is a big span, so when she got into high school, Michael and I spent a lot of time together because our focus was swimming. In our younger years, I remember going rollerblading and playing hoops with him and teaching him how to mow the grass."

Whitney never minded the extra time with Michael because, especially when she got into high school, she realized and appreciated even more how much their mother gave to them and sacrificed to be able to provide for them.

"I took him under my wing, because my mom being a single parent took a lot—she was a teacher, so in the summers she took summer jobs to make ends meet," Whitney said. "A lot of times, Michael and I would bum around together, going to the pool or hanging around the house. He would often go off and play with friends or play video games. During those times and for school, I'd make him breakfast, get him on the bus—just caring for him. Certainly there were times when he was obnoxious and annoying, not always perfect, but I'm sure he'd say the same about me."

Whitney, who said she believes everyone in the

family has ADHD to varying degrees, though not as severely as Michael, said she too prefers to be busy.

"I think if I didn't have those things (family and work), I would not know what to do with myself," she said. "I do better in a chaotic setting. The more responsibilities I have, the better I am."

While Michael and his mother were always very close, Debbie Phelps is also close to her daughters.

"She's incredibly strong, and a wonderful woman," Hilary said. "She has always instilled in her children, just like her mother did with her, that everyone is equal—no one person is better than another, and you treat all with the same kindness that you would treat a friend. We are all humble and giving, and that comes from Mom. She taught us how to make decisions, and also to live with the consequences of our decisions. She would, and still does, talk through options with us, weighing the outcomes and consequences, until we come to a decision that we think is best. I'm sure it was hard for her when we made decisions that didn't match up with what she thought, but she let us make them and live with the results. But she was always there to talk through issues or concerns that stemmed from the decision."

With three children—all of whom were in sports—Whitney appreciates the time their mother took to make sure the children never suffered from being in a single-parent household.

"She's an amazing woman," Whitney said. "She had three young kids, raised them on her own, and remember, we all three swam, at different levels. So that meant different practice times, caps, goggles, swimsuits and travel meets. We were a busy bunch. Then we started driving, so there were cars and gas and insurance. Kids take a lot of time—she gave up a lot of herself for us."

Chapter 2

The Family That Swims Together: The Push to 2000 for the Phelps Siblings

Whitney had her own disorder to overcome.

Back pain started for Whitney when she was just a ten-year-old age-group swimmer. By age twelve, according to a *Swimming World Magazine* article from November 2005, the pain was so bad that she could not always practice, and two years later, she was in pain every single day. She was still able to win Nationals in the 200 butterfly, which would become one of her brother's signature events and the first in which he'd make the Olympic team in 2000. She had a herniated disc and two bulging discs in her back.

Whitney won a bronze medal in Rome at the World Championships. Unable to train as vigorously, she thought losing weight would help her.

"I thought if I could be thinner," she told *Swimming World*, "I could be more fit—and everything would be okay."

She did lose some weight, and, coincidentally or not, she was able to train more, and became a compulsive exerciser and stopped eating certain things altogether.

By the 1995 Pan-Pacific Championships in Atlanta, the city that would host the 1996 Summer Olympics, a team manager talked to Debbie Phelps, who said she had already taken Whitney to a nutritionist, according to *Swimming World*. Others were noticing how thin Whitney had become. Her coach, Murray Stephens of North Baltimore Aquatic Club, also talked to her, and would even stand nearby and watch to make sure Whitney ate a bagel and cream cheese before he would let her practice.

Whitney still managed to be seeded first in the 200 butterfly for the U.S. at the time of the 1996 Olympic Trials, and was ranked third in the world. Though she made the finals, she finished sixth, not making the top two spots, which earned berths on the Olympic team.

She continued to lose weight, and finally ended up seeking help to deal with the disorder.

Stephens, who took charge of NBAC in 2008 and had not a decade earlier hired Bob Bowman and the other coaches who have continued NBAC's strong tradition, took the lessons he learned from Whitney in 1996 to heart. He made sure the coaches, swimmers, and their parents knew about the need to eat properly, and to be on the lookout for any swimmer, particularly girls, who were not getting enough nutrition or suddenly lost a lot of weight.

Like Michael and Whitney, Hilary swam for North Baltimore Aquatic Club. Whereas Whitney swam for UNLV in college, Hilary earned a scholarship to the University of Richmond in nearby Virginia.

"I swam for NBAC for close to ten years before heading off to college," Hilary said. "I swam for the University of Richmond, which is a Division I school, all four years. I had a few school records, but they are long gone. There have been girls who came through after I graduated that were really fast. Like Michael and Whitney, I swam the 200 butterfly, but I mostly swam distance. Breaststroke was my least favorite, but I liked swimming distance."

Before the Olympics Trials, Michael Phelps had an injury of his own to deal with. His case was documented in an article on USA Swimming's Web site. Like many great swimmers before him, he had shoulder pain that prevented him from swimming with the correct form.

The Phelpses were referred to a respected local physical therapist, Scott Heinlein, by former Olympian Anita Nall. Heinlein, in a subsequent interview, noted that Michael also had some lower back pain. Michael was just fourteen years old at the time and had grown six inches during the previous year. While the actual pain was a concern, even more so was the instability that Heinlein wrote was an underlying problem. The injury was treated with two treatment sessions, called "manipulations," and within a week Phelps was better.

"There was a pain in the shoulder and there was a shifting," Phelps was quoted as saying in the report. "It was like a ball rolling back and forth. The pain was on the top of the shoulder, a little to the front, and the shifting was in the back. I could feel it shifting when I was in the pool, like my muscles weren't strong enough to handle what was going on. Every time I took a stroke I could feel the shifting in my shoulder. It was like shifting gears . . . regular to shift, regular to shift. It wasn't smooth at all. Like going from old pavement to new pavement. And it only hurt on free and fly. We weren't doing too much dry-land back then, but I couldn't do pull-ups. I had to do smaller amounts. I couldn't do the pull-ups because of the shoulder."

Bowman had been unsure whether Phelps was really hurt or not—he could see him swimming without the usual form and technique.

"Maybe he had a problem, but I didn't know for sure," Bowman said. "I spent all of practice that day playing the little game, 'What's wrong?' 'Nothing.' Michael waited until the end of practice to tell me about the shoulder. I knew something wasn't right, but he wouldn't admit to it when I asked. I don't think he did more damage to it, but if it had been more serious, he might have."

Phelps said the injury helped him learn a valuable lesson, one he'd apply in the future, especially when he had lower back problems between 2004 and 2008 that required him to visit the physical therapist again and get treatment.

"Don't skip practice or avoid telling your coach when your shoulder hurts," Phelps said in the report. "Tell him or her right away. Trying to hide it might make it worse."

Bowman agreed.

"Just ask—if you know there is something wrong, go through your checklist: Are you feeling well? How are your shoulders?" Bowman said. "Based on the attitude of the swimmer, you'll know what to ask. Of course, it depends who you're dealing with. But if it's someone who hates to miss practice, keep asking the questions. Seek medical advice immediately. One of the greatest assets is having someone who can see the athlete right away. Not next Tuesday—tomorrow. If something is really bad, this is necessary. If it's a growth issue or a flexibility problem, it can wait. But if it's going to impact the training program, immediate help is critical. There has to be an open channel of communication."

Whitney was at the 2000 U.S. Olympic Trials—

she had a qualifying time—when Michael made his first Olympic team in the 200 butterfly, which had been his sister's specialty event.

"Being on deck when Michael made the 2000 team" was a good memory, Whitney said. "Because I had made the 2000 Olympic Trials but I pulled out because of my back, so I was on deck when he made the team, and I was able to hug him and congratulate him."

However, Whitney was not there to see her brother swim at the 2000 Olympics in Sydney, Australia.

"I didn't go—I was going to school [at UNLV] in Vegas, but I did watch him race on TV," Whitney said. "I was very proud of him, but I was going through a tough time. Due to my injury I had to stop swimming and I was having a hard time accepting that. It took me a year or two to come to terms with everything. Now I really enjoy watching Michael and am so proud of all of his accomplishments."

Michael remembers the 2000 Sydney Olympics, and how all the experiences from that trip shaped his future. The other swimmer in the 200 butterfly was Tom Malchow, a University of Michigan swimmer. Malchow, who had a hard time dealing with shoulder injuries as well, especially in the years to come, won the gold medal in Sydney. Phelps made the final and took fifth place, a solid Olympic debut.

"What I learned in 2000 has helped me become a

better swimmer and a better person," Michael said. "Being fifteen and being in that kind of spotlight completely changed me and helped me do the things I've done since then."

Whitney still swims, kickboxes and does spin classes. Whitney, who has since married and changed her name to Whitney Flickinger, and her husband have two children, daughter Taylor and son Connor.

"It is challenging. It is rewarding. It's hard at times, because I'm a full-time mom and I have a full-time job," Whitney said. "There's never a dull moment, but I love every second of it. To watch my kids grow and see my kids' faces, it is just great to be a part of such amazing things every day with them."

Whitney has seen the ups and downs of competitive swimming, both for herself and her brother. She said it's her kids' decision as to whether they will become swimmers. She said both of her children love the water.

"They are happy in the pool, and throw a fit when they have to come out," Whitney said. "If Taylor and Connor want to go on to swim, great. If not, that's fine—whatever they choose to do."

While Whitney's back problems took her away from swimming for good, Hilary enjoys it as a way to stay in shape, and she's inspired by her brother.

"I swim occasionally," Hilary said. "After every one of Michael's meets, I am compelled to start back up with training again. I competed in a triathlon a few years ago, and have entertained that thought of doing another one. I still swim a few times a month and find the water very comforting. But I mostly do yoga. And living in the city, I do a lot of walking."

Chapter 3

The Architect Behind the Plan: Coach Bob Bowman

When discussing Michael Phelps, one has to discuss his coach, Bob Bowman. The two are now rarely separated in the world of swimming, but Bob had coached for a long time before he met the Phelpses or became a national team coach.

Many of the U.S. Olympic swim team coaches have been long-time college coaches, like Mark Schubert, who is now head of all the USA Swimming national teams. The 2008 head men's coach, Eddie Reese, had already been an Olympic coach, and now guides the University of Texas men's team. His charges include the "big three"—Ian Crocker, Aaron Peirsol, and Brendan Hansen, along with relay swimmers David Walters and Ricky Berens. The 2008 U.S. head women's coach, Jack Bauerle, is the head coach at the University of Georgia. Certainly many club coaches have made names for themselves on national, and even Olympic, teams.

Bob Bowman came into the sport as a club coach. The program he started coaching—and the program that Michael Phelps came up through—is the North Baltimore Aquatic Club, home to countless Olympians and medal winners.

Bowman swam for Florida State University from 1983 to 1985. He majored in developmental psychology and earned a minor in music composition. He still spends some time playing the piano, which he maintains a passion for, though he claims it is something he could never do professionally.

"I play the piano—it's definitely not a second career, but it's something that I really enjoy," Bowman said.

While finishing his degree, Bowman coached age-group swimmers at the Area Tallahassee Aquatic Club, and also served as an assistant coach at Florida State. But a year after graduating, he moved on to be an assistant coach for a club team in Las Vegas, Nevada, for two years. He then coached as an assistant from 1990 to 1991 in Cincinnati for another club team, and then moved on to California, where he was again an assistant coach, this time the Napa Valley Swim Team (1991–1992). Known for being a strict disciplinarian in and out of the water, Bowman had a solid career as a swimmer before becoming a coach.

"I was a strong Junior National swimmer," Bowman said, adding with a smile, "and yes, I was probably overly disciplined."

From 1992 to 1994, Bowman moved to the Birmingham Swim League, serving as head coach and program director, building the program into a top five national powerhouse. He returned in 1994 to Napa Valley as head coach, where the program had an elite group of National Team and National Junior Team swimmers. In 1996, he moved to North Baltimore Aquatic Club, serving three years as senior coach before moving up to high performance coach in 1999. He won several national coaching awards.

While he was in Sydney in 2000 for Michael Phelps' Olympic debut in the 200 butterfly, Bowman was not an official coach for the U.S. team. But in 2004, he was named an assistant U.S. Olympic men's coach, and Phelps won six gold medals and two bronze medals.

As an athlete, Bowman was also a standout high school football player. He played center on offense and nose tackle on defense, and loved both the thinking and the collisions that came with every snap of the ball. But when Michael talked about going out for high school football, Bowman steered his star swimmer away from that idea. Knowing that Phelps was built perfectly for a swimmer, his tall, lean physique would have taken a beating on the football field. Phelps also considered going out for golf in high school briefly, but with his swimming schedule, the links did not fit into the program.

Bowman said one of his favorite sayings is, "No one cares how much you know until they know how much you care." That saying guided Bowman's approach, which included taking personal responsibility for and designing the program that Michael would follow for more than a decade to come.

Bowman satisfies his need for speed in another way—horse racing. He has been a successful horse trainer in addition to the accolades he has gained as a swim coach. He said if there was one place he could pick to live—with swimming not being a factor—he would have loved to live in Lexington, Kentucky.

If he weren't a swim coach, Bowman said, "I'd be training horses at Churchill Downs. Yes, Churchill Downs—I wouldn't want to play in the minor leagues." He went on to add that his favorite movie is *Seabiscuit*. But Bowman pointed out that Baltimore has great horse racing, something he takes time to enjoy and participate in when time allows.

Taking over coaching for Michael when he was eleven years old, Bowman right away saw something special, and a bond was built between swimmer and coach that would guide them through three Olympics and more gold medals than any swimmer had ever won.

Michael said that Bowman reminded him of a

drill sergeant. But Bowman knows who his military role model would be.

"General Patton," Bowman said. "He was pretty intense."

Bowman said knowing his swimmers individually is as important as the swim routine he designs, and that knowing his swimmers helps him design those programs.

"The main thing now is what it has been for any generation: trying to know what motivates each athlete," Bowman said. "You have to treat them as individuals within a group setting. You need to take care of each athlete. That's the most important thing you have to do for significant change to take place—to help the individual where she or he needs to be helped."

Not only does Bowman know Phelps well, the star swimmer knows his coach just as well. They are so close that they both know how to get under each other's skin.

"It's one of those things that sometimes makes it work, or sometimes might not make it work," Bowman said. "Sometimes I wish he didn't know me so well, because he can push my buttons like no other and vice versa, right? But we're so close right now that we communicate on a level that the typical coach and athlete cannot. I can watch him swim in warm-ups, know what he's doing, give him a hand signal, and he knows what I'm saying."

While Bowman has been to several Olympics now, he says one Olympics in particular would have been breathtaking to take in, in person.

"I would have liked to go to the 1976 Olympics in Montreal, where the [American] men won virtually every gold medal," Bowman said. "They didn't win just one event, the 200 breaststroke."

While Phelps is amazing, Bowman said there could be another. That athlete, however, could be wearing soccer cleats, holding a tennis racquet or golf club, or shooting a basketball.

"The Michael Phelpses are out there," Bowman said. "The problem swimming has is we have those kinds of athletes out there, but maybe we lose them to other sports. Maybe in seeing Michael's performance, we will see them stay with swimming."

He knows who else he would have liked to coach—U.S. women's star Tracy Caulkins, who dominated the world in every event, something not done since. Bowman imagines she would have been the perfect pupil.

"Tracy Caulkins would have been great to coach, because she's such a nice person," Bowman said. "I can't imagine she'd be hard to deal with. She also has unbelievable talent. Of course some people would say I'm coaching the male version of that now."

Caulkins said reading Bowman's comments about her meant a lot.

"I am very flattered that I am still referred to after all these years, and it is nice to be remembered after all these years," Caulkins said. "I had some great coaches and would have loved to have been coached by Bob, and trained with Michael."

Taking the head coaching job at the University of Michigan in 2004, where he'd stay through the 2008 Olympics before returning as CEO at North Baltimore, was an easy move to make because his roots were so established in Baltimore, plus it had the horse racing that is such an enjoyable part of his life.

"I just felt like I had accomplished a lot of things at North Baltimore," Bowman said. "When I had the opportunity to come to Michigan, after meeting the people and getting a feel for where I needed to be— it's hard to put your finger on, but I had kind of a gut reaction that this was the right place for me."

Though Bowman's intensity isn't always correctly perceived by some, Phelps understands his coach perfectly, and appreciates Bowman's passion.

"It is always very, very tense—it is just how he is," Phelps said. "I was warned about that from an early stage of my career. He just wants us to do our best and he wants the best for us. He loves what he does."

Phelps' estranged relationship with his own father, retired Maryland State Trooper Fred Phelps, has been well documented. Though Michael has talked to his father on occasion, they are more "off" in an on-again, off-again relationship. It was Michael who gave away his sister Whitney at her wedding, in fact.

Michigan treated Phelps and Bowman right from the get-go. At the Michigan-Iowa football games in 2004, all the Olympians from the university were honored in a pre-game ceremony, including Coach Bowman, who said coaching at a major public university helped him immerse himself in a college culture that he hadn't been a part of in more than a decade.

"One of the true joys of being on a college campus is all the activities," Bowman said. "I'll also attend concerts at the Hill Auditorium, one of the best acoustic venues in the nation. When [acts] come to the United States, they go to New York, L.A., but they also include Ann Arbor because of the impressive venue. There's a lot of things to do here—that's why I love it, because it's not just a place for swimming."

Olympian Erik Vendt went to Michigan to train under Bowman at Club Wolverine. He said Bowman had clearly adapted his style to dealing with older swimmers.

"I think he has a different way with us post-grad guys than with the college kids," Vendt said. "What I understand is that he is different now than he was at North Baltimore because he's working with an older group. If I was twelve years old and training for him, I'd be under a much tighter grip. But as post-grads, we have some autonomy."

Peter Vanderkaay, another 2004 Olympian, said

Bowman was a big change from Jon Urbanchek, the former Michigan coach, but that the change of pace kept the program headed in the right direction.

"He loves developing swimmers," Vanderkaay said of Bowman. "And I think he's found his niche."

Adapting to college coaching included mastering the NCAA-regulated recruiting process. Bowman quickly found recruiting took up as much or more time than coaching at particular times of the year, and was a constant responsibility he had to attend to as head coach.

"The biggest difference [from club to college] is the recruiting and the energy that goes into it," Bowman said. "Not that we didn't in club [swimming] but nothing compared to what we do here. The similarities are that the guys I have here are very hard-working and want to get better, so that's very similar to North Baltimore."

Bowman learned early that finding good swimmers was not only what he was looking for when he started to build recruiting classes.

"The challenge for recruiting is finding the athletes who have the swimming ability we want, and secondly, also fit in with our team concept and work ethic and have the same vision," Bowman said. "Thirdly and probably most important, finding student-athletes who meet the high academic standards here: We're looking for very good athletes who are very good students."

He also believes recruiting made him a better coach.

"One of the things I love is to go out recruiting and see the other programs," Bowman said. "This affords me the opportunity to watch some great coaches coach. I also really enjoy traveling and doing the home visits."

Another key to Bowman's transition was that the coach who had just retired from Michigan, Jon Urbanchek, another former Olympic coach, stayed around town and was nothing but a positive influence in Bowman's start at Michigan. In fact, Bowman dropped thirty pounds jogging with Urbanchek each morning, during which time the two coaches would talk about athletes and training programs.

"Jon gives me a lot of guidance," Bowman said. "We run together almost every day. I keep him abreast of things. And he gives me a lot of advice—who to talk to, where to go. He's just a great person and coach. It's a very unique situation because we've known each other for a long time. Jon is, quite frankly, one of the nicest people I've ever known. He doesn't have a mean bone in his body."

Running with Urbanchek not only brought down Bowman's weight, it also helped him manage his mental outlook.

"It makes me handle stress a lot better," Bowman said. "Running helps me make better decisions about training, and keeps me from getting frustrated as much."

Bowman immediately raised the level of swimming at Michigan. He coached both the University of Michigan team and the elite swimmers at Club Wolverine, which is made of age-group swimmers and professionals, mostly former Olympians and National Team members who had at least competed at World Championships. World Championships are held every other year (in odd-numbered-ending years).

"I think it has been an easier transition than I thought, and I credit it to a couple of things: the administration at Michigan has been fantastic in providing a lot of help for me to get up to speed and knowing the rules," Bowman said. "The second thing was the support I've gotten from [former Michigan coach] Jon Urbanchek, who has really supported me and helped me out with advice. He's been a real positive influence and a key element in the transition going so well. I can't thank him enough."

Bowman has heard several of his swimmers comment publicly about how well the transition went.

"It does make me feel pretty good because the most important thing we do as coaches is communicate," Bowman said. "If you can't get your message across or hear what the athletes are saying, I don't think it works. It's good to know they feel they are getting good coaching. These are great athletes and they are already motivated. So I can move full speed ahead since I don't have to worry about them getting on board the train. They already are on board before I even start."

While Bowman had been to plenty of big national and international meets, including a pair of Olympics, he said the conference competition in college swimming was even more passionate than he had heard it was.

"I will be perfectly honest—I was not prepared for what the Big Ten meet would be like emotionally," Bowman said. "The intensity level was much higher than I thought."

Having so many Olympians in practice made workouts as exciting to watch for swim aficionados as many meets.

"It is pretty competitive, and it's fun," Bowman said. "One of the things I would say—Jon and I joke about this quite a bit—is that only two or three of them are ready to go like that on a given day, and the others are on the next day, so it's rare that all six or seven or eight are all like that, but when they are, it's something to behold."

Yet the college schedule, dotted with dual meets and invites before a conference championship and then the NCAA Championship meet, wasn't much more grueling than a typical year coaching elite club swimmers.

"It really isn't any more chaotic where I am now compared to where I was, because you get a general plan and see where people are going," Bowman said. "Once you know their competition schedule, you work backward from there to their daily training plans. Besides, I like being busy—I'm a good multi-tasker."

Michigan's high level of accomplishment—on the athletic field, in the classroom, and in the "real world"—stimulated Bowman intellectually.

"I love the attitude of the people, and there's always an infectious enthusiasm about the future," Bowman said. "I like the high standards and how everyone at this university wants to be the best, whether it's in the classroom, doing research, or making a positive impact."

Oddly, the coach whose entire mantra is preparation finds his swimmers seem to do the best when his own stomach is filled with butterflies.

"The irony is that I have always found the meets where we do the best are the ones where I doubt myself beforehand," Bowman said.

Whitney Phelps, Michael's sister who was a U.S. National team member and just missed making the 1996 Olympic team and also qualified for Olympic Trials in 2000 but had to withdraw because of injuries, said Bowman was the right coach for Michael from the first time they met.

"Bob has watched Michael go from a young boy to a man," Whitney said. "Bob has been working with Michael since he was ten or eleven years old. He had been in the sport for some time at that point. They work together because they understood each other. Bob respects Michael and Michael respects Bob. As Michael got older and got some independence, they butted heads, but at the end of the day, they'd come back together and move on. Bob has definitely been a big part of Michael's life, and he's been a big part of our family. Some coaches and swimmers butt heads and it doesn't work out. But Michael and Bob work well together. Over the years there have been many swimmers that have trained under Bob and he has done an excellent job with all levels of athletes."

Chapter 4

Quest for History, Take 1: Athens, 2004

The problems were logistical, both with the meet being completely around the world in Sydney, Australia, and also with the media. After settling for a bronze early in the Games, on the second day of events the media horde following Phelps' quest to match Mark Spitz dwindled to a trickle. Even Phelps and Coach Bob Bowman noted that Michael was doing the 200 freestyle with an eye to the future, not thinking about winning a gold medal in the present competing against the world-record-holding Aussie, Ian Thorpe, there in his prime.

Phelps started the Australia Games by breaking the world record in the 400 IM (Individual Medley), with blue-collared Erik Vendt taking the silver. In fact, Phelps' reaction after seeing that his teammate had taken second was to reach over the lane lines and hold up a tired Vendt's left arm in victory.

"It is a big honor for America to win two medals in the 400 IM," Phelps said, enthusiastic about the one-two finish.

Coach Bob Bowman, appearing to be calm, admitted later that he had more nerves than Phelps.

"I will tell you, I felt nervous for Michael's first final—the 400 IM," Bowman said. "I faked calm for that and tried to make myself smile—I felt like I could throw up until he got that done with. After that, I got into a calmer mindset."

Michael's sister, Whitney, a former swimmer herself, was there just outside the fence that surrounded the pool deck, and got to see up close her brother's first win and first Olympic gold medal.

"After Michael won his first gold—that was the 400 IM—I was able to talk to him afterward through the fence, just congratulating him, touching his medal, and talking with him," Whitney said of the memory.

The Americans were favored to do better than the bronze medal they earned the next day in the 4×100 freestyle relay. Ian Crocker, who had been sick, swam the leadoff leg, followed by Phelps, Neil Walker and sprinter Jason Lezak. The South Africans won with a world record of 3:13.17, with the Netherlands placing second at 3:14.36. The Americans were a disappointing third, at 3:14.62.

With eight teams in the final, and four swimmers per country, only Crocker went above fifty seconds for his 100-meter leg of the relay. Crocker had qualified for the 100 freestyle as an individual at the Trials, winning one of the two coveted spots in the event. He had proven he was capable four short weeks before, but there was no test for the coaches to know who was in the best shape of the top two places individually. The other four relay qualifiers had raced in the preliminary heats to determine who would be fastest. The individual 100 freestyle wasn't until later in the meet, so Crocker and Lezak were as yet untested in the competition.

Bowman said putting Crocker on the relay was not a mistake.

"In my opinion you go with who you think will be the four fastest people on a given night," Bowman said. "That's the way we [the Olympic coaches] did it. There's not a computer program that's going to tell you who is best. Ultimately, the coach has to use his experience, his staff, and make that judgment."

Phelps did his leg in 48.74, while Neil Walker blazed in at 47.97, and Lezak had the best leg at 47.86 for the Americans. Lezak was faster than any of the four South Africans. Crocker, four weeks before at the Olympic Trials, had swum a time of 49.06 to qualify for the individual 100 freestyle. Certainly, a second faster time from Crocker and half a second better by Phelps would have given the Americans the gold by .05 over South Africa. But it wasn't meant to be. U.S. media interest in swimming waned. Of course, Lezak would shatter his own best time in 2008, going 46.06 seconds as the United States reclaimed the world record with a time of 3:08.24. But in Athens in 2004, all the Americans felt after the 4×100 freestyle relay was frustration.

The swimming world was calling the 200 freestyle "The Race of the Century" at the 2004 Athens Games, as the final had the four fastest men in the event in history. Thorpe had held the world record, Pieter van den Hoogenband had won gold in the event at the 2000 Sydney Olympics, Australian Grant Hackett previously had the world record, and Phelps, who had already recorded a time to make him among the world's best in an event where he was just beginning to develop his talent. Thorpe won, followed by Hoogenband, and Phelps came away with another bronze medal, so his quest was shifted to trying to finish the Games with six gold medals.

"I did what I wanted to do," Phelps said. "I did my best time, and I raced the two greatest 200-meter swimmers of all time, so I am happy."

Still, the bronze in the 200 freestyle, an event that was not his specialty at the time gained him a lot of respect.

"That 200 free was a long shot for a win," Bowman said. "Yet I thought that was his best performance out of everything."

Phelps was back on top of the podium in his next individual event, the 200 butterfly, winning with an Olympic record time of 1:54.04, a half second ahead of his nearest competitor, giving him two gold medals and two bronze medals at that point.

That same day, Phelps and the United States burned off an American record to claim gold in the 4×200 freestyle relay. Phelps teamed with Ryan Lochte, Peter Vanderkaay, and Klete Keller to finish at 7:07.33, just thirteen one-hundredths ahead of second-place Australia. Keller held off Australian superstar Ian Thorpe on the final leg to give the Americans gold.

Back in his element for his other specialty event, the 200 IM, Phelps blew to a win by 1.64 seconds over American teammate Lochte, who took silver. That gave Phelps four golds and two bronze medals with two events remaining, the 100 butterfly and 4×100 medley relay.

Bowman made careful mental notes with an eye toward what program Phelps would put together for 2008.

"Oh, absolutely, he was tired—I probably noticed it about halfway through" the Games, Bowman said. "It's very interesting: when you are in the middle of that, those long days and long nights . . . it was only day four, and I had to think, 'We're halfway through.' But it seems like those four days were longer than the training camp and even Olympic Trials combined."

The 100 fly would not be an easy race, and his best competition was a familiar face, Ian Crocker, the world record-holder in the event. Phelps was just four one-hundredths of a second better, going 51.25 to Crocker's 51.29 to give Phelps his fifth gold medal.

Relays are set up so more than four swimmers qualify and are allowed to compete to get through the preliminary heat. Phelps swam the preliminary butterfly leg for the medley relay. By beating Crocker, he also earned the right to swim in the final. But saying the team came to Athens as a "team" and would leave as one, he yielded his spot. Phelps, with his win in the 100 fly, had the option to race in the final of the medley relay. Instead, he gave his spot to Crocker, who competed in the final. The team of Peirsol, Hansen, Crocker, and Lezak had experience on their side, not only from the NCAA level at Texas, but at the previous three national team events, like the world championships or Pan-Pacific games, each year. The Americans, with Phelps cheering on from the stands, won the gold medal and broke the world record. As part of the prelim team, Michael picked up his sixth gold medal to go along with his pair of bronze medals, a total of eight medals at the 2004 Games. Crocker also earned his medley relay gold by helping his teammates best the field.

In 2004, the Americans had a great showing, bringing home many medals and records. But Phelps' act of giving up that relay spot to a teammate was arguably the most memorable and talked-about moment of the Games. Phelps, who had been considered a "lone wolf," listening to his iPod before races and keeping to himself, showed a level of class and consideration for his teammates that set him apart. With the 400 medley relay as the last swimming event of the Olympics, Phelps was remembered with respect, even as he looked forward to four years from that point.

Phelps used the success in 2004 and built on it to set himself up for how he would approach 2008.

"Go in and have fun," Phelps said. "If I do better—and I'd love to do better than I did in Athens—that would be great. But the most important thing is to try as hard as I can and have fun with it. That's what I did in Athens, so I will go into 2008 with the same motto—to make the team, have fun, and do my best."

Bowman had no complaints with Phelps' performance in Athens.

"I would say he did everything I thought he could do," Bowman said. "Coach Bowman: I would personally sleep more. I don't know that I'd do anything differently. The great thing about how I feel now is I'm sure there are things ... maybe I could've changed some training things. But you always look back and think you could do something better. I'd probably go back and work on some technical details—but then what would I be saying now [if] I would've sacrificed to draw the focus to those things? The great thing about Michael and me is I know we have no regrets, that looking back we did everything to be ready and the results speak for themselves."

In November 2004, Phelps was charged with drunk driving. He was pulled over with a couple of friends in the car. The state trooper who stopped him smelled alcohol and thought that Phelps looked intoxicated. Phelps at first denied it, then admitted it after a field sobriety test, saying he was sorry for lying but he was "scared" because he had a "lot to lose."

"I recognize the seriousness of this mistake. I've learned from this mistake and will continue learning from this mistake for the rest of my life," Phelps said in court.

Phelps pleaded guilty to driving while impaired, and as part of the deal (called common by the prosecutor), charges of driving under the influence, underage drinking, and failure to stop at a stop sign were dropped. His blood level was tested at .08, exactly the legal limit in Maryland.

Phelps received eighteen months of probation, had to talk to school kids about the dangers of drinking and driving, and attend a Mothers Against Drunk Driving victim-impact panel.

Phelps never shied away from responsibility for the mistake. Ironically, Davis R. Ruark, the state attorney for Wicomico County, Maryland, who prosecuted Phelps, was arrested for drunk driving in 2008. He pleaded guilty, got unsupervised probation, and an accompanying charge of "handgun possession while under the influence" was dropped as part of his plea agreement.

Chapter 5

Becoming a Young Man: Life at the University of Michigan

When Bob Bowman came back to North Baltimore Aquatic Club from the Athens Olympics in 2004, it seemed as though he and Michael would gather, regroup, and decide a new plan of action to once again try to match Mark Spitz's record of seven gold medals. But Bowman made a decision at that point to take his career in a direction away from the comforts of what they had both called home. Long-time Michigan coach and legend, Jon Urbanchek, had retired, and Michigan athletic director, Bill Martin, a USOC board member, hired Bowman to replace Urbanchek.

So Michael Phelps, who never had made any formal plans for college, went with Bowman to Michigan.

Already nineteen years old, Phelps was going off

to college to be around young men and women his own age and slightly older, and would live on his own for the first time as well. It was a move that Phelps' sister, Whitney, welcomed.

"I think it's something all kids need to do; they need to get away from their parents and home," Whitney said. "For the longest time it had been my mother and him—her doing the cooking and the laundry. She took care of him, and made sure he was up for practice. She made sure he got home from practice okay, made sure he did his school work. Michael needed to be away from home, make his own choices—good and bad choices, because you learn from the choices you make."

Hilary agreed.

"I think it's helped Michael to learn responsibility," Hilary said. "He's a very responsible person in general, but moving away from home taught him how to take care of himself. If he was out of milk, he had to go and buy some more. We are a very protective family, and very protective of Michael, but I think this helped him develop into his own person."

Michael said the time on his own helped him learn how to deal with the day-to-day vagaries of adulthood.

"I started learning a lot of things about being on your own," Michael said. "Making my own food obviously involves going to the grocery store. I make a lot of pasta, chicken, and steak. There's a variety there. About the cooking, listen, sometimes it's not always good! This is the first time I have had to really cook for myself, things like dinner, so I'm learning—sometimes the hard way—how to do it. I don't always get it right."

Phelps said at the time that he liked Michigan, and found the camaraderie of a college program something he enjoyed.

"One of the biggest things I've found here is that as a team, Michigan is really close, almost like family away from home," Michael said. "It's a good group to be able to go to every day."

Phelps was also excited to be in school for the first time he could remember. He hadn't enjoyed the academic part of high school that much, and after going professional as a swimmer and giving up his college eligibility, he hadn't made firm plans back in Baltimore to start his college education.

"I'll say this: It's the first time I'm really interested about my classes and excited to go to class to learn new stuff," Phelps said. "I'm in classes I want to be in, classes that I enjoy."

But he found that schoolwork took a lot of time out of his routine, especially as it related to traveling for sponsorship appearances. After less than a handful of classes, Phelps shut it down academically and focused on swimming.

While he was relatively well-known in Balti-more, the major metropolitan area still allowed him, at least until 2004, to go around the city relatively anonymously. Such was not the case in Michigan.

"I'm recognized—actually people recognize me here more than they did in Baltimore, because Ann Arbor is a smaller city, almost a town atmosphere," Phelps said.

The biggest adjustment was not being around Debbie Phelps, who for much of Michael's life had been, along with his sisters, his primary support system.

"It's different—it's interesting," Michael said. "But it's a change that was needed because I was starting to grow up more. We still talk weekly and she comes and visits a lot. We still have that close-ness even though we're not in same household."

Phelps said that training with the college pro-gram had helped him get physically stronger.

"I think just a variety of different things," Phelps said of what has worked well for him. "I have never lifted a single weight [before Michigan]. So I think doing different kinds of training will help me."

He also got to train at Michigan with several Olympians, including Peter Vanderkaay, Chris Thompson, and eventually Erik Vendt, who came later to Ann Arbor. Michigan was also home to hopefuls like Davis Tarwater and Chris DeJong.

"They are normal guys," Phelps said. "Peter is down-to-earth, not real outgoing unless you know him, but a good guy who loves training. Davis is always funny, a joker during workouts, always talking in a good mood. He's always singing old songs during workouts."

Klete Keller, the colorful, wonderfully eccentric Olympian, was also at Club Wolverine when Phelps got there.

"Klete is one of a kind, I think—he's not the 'normal person,' but he's definitely someone good to have around," Phelps said. "He's funny and outgoing. He's a guy I love to be around."

Though Coach Bowman expected Michael to thrive in the environment, he credited Phelps and his teammates for making it work so well shortly after the pair moved to Michigan.

"It's worked out really well," Bowman said. "A lot of that is Michael, and a lot of that is the team. When you get down to it, Michael's a regular guy who does wonderful things. He just fits in very well. We have a lot of people in this program pulling in the same direction—people like Michael, Klete, Peter, Chris DeJong, Chris Thompson, Davis Tarwater—so to have all of these great swimmers adds to the excitement."

When Vendt joined the club leading up to the 2008 preparation, Kaitlin Sandeno, an Olympic medalist, also made the trek with Vendt from USC to Michigan. Phelps welcomed Vendt, who is known as one of the hardest training partners in the sport.

One of the more interesting swimmers on the 2008 team, Erik Vendt had pondered joining the Navy SEALS after 9/11. The 2000 Olympic swimmer did not join the service after pausing to reflect, and came back to make the Olympic team in 2004. He was outstanding again in the Athens Games. A distance ace, he had finished second to Phelps in the 400 IM, grabbing a silver medal.

Vendt turned to an organic diet after 2004 and recommitted to swimming, and was pleased to be doing his best times.

"I think it's the consistency in the training," Vendt said. "My strength is getting better. I'm able to focus my life on swimming. All of those reasons have an equal importance."

He trained for two of the hardest, most militaristically styled coaches in the sport, Mark Schubert at USC, and Bob Bowman at Michigan for the lead-up to 2008.

"They have a reputation for giving you the most yardage and so forth, but that works for me," Vendt said. "I feel the most comfortable with that kind of training."

September 11 was already a special day in the Vendt family, albeit for a very different reason.

"It has a weird personal side to it, because it's my sister's birthday," Vendt said. "Also, it's very personal because I have really good friends who are in the service, and I think about them on a day like [that]. I get emotional, but for a different reason than people think. My three good friends are serving. That's what I am thinking about."

But after that initial response after the 2000 Olympics to enlist or go through officer training, Vendt had opened his mind to the world and taken stock of all the facts, with emotion taking a suitable but smaller role in his perspective.

"The freshness and horror of the moment was stuck in my mind for a while," Vendt said. "Fortunately or unfortunately, it's starting to go away a little with time, though I won't forget what happened. But like I said, I have friends fighting in this war, so 9/11 does mean something extra."

Vendt returned from Athens, and turned around and went out into the world. He explored New Zealand, Australia, and Tahiti. He returned to America to finish his degree at USC—he had just one class left. Then he took off for Europe and backpacked for more than three months, hitting all the major cities, a lot of little-known places, too. That trip with a group of non-Americans got Vendt to thinking— about what he thought, and about other points of view.

"I was gung-ho—I am still proud to be an American," Vendt said. "I freely admit that I have changed, but it's in a good way. Traveling to Europe makes you see a different way of life, and just because people don't see things our way doesn't mean they are wrong. I took all of these experiences and cultures from other people I met, and it has taught me a lot about other walks of life. It taught me a lot about myself, and our country, too. I was thinking about going into the service, and when I got back to New York, I realized that wasn't for me, even though I respect those who serve. We just need to know about the world more, and understand other cultures better. There's so much more out there we need to know and understand. I really did a lot of soul-searching, met a lot of people, and came to a lot of conclusions."

That break not only refocused Vendt on who he was as a person and an American, but what he could still be as a swimmer.

"Taking a break really did a lot for me, for my mind and my body," Vendt said. "It made me fall in love with the sport again, and for the right reason. That kind of outlook has done well for me. You know, I saw these great places, these great sites, the Vatican and these amazing beaches," Vendt said. "But the people, the culture, learning about the rest of this world is what I treasure."

He met a lot of people from different countries—Italian, French and Australian friends he still stays in touch with—and expressed his own thoughts. But mostly he listened, and spent time thinking.

"When you travel [to] Europe and stay in these hostels, you meet so many people," Vendt said. "The common bond is this love of travel and of culture. I met so many amazing people, and we had these immediate connections. I can't even describe to you how fantastic the people were, just across the board. We had these great talks. I learned so much. It opened my eyes to the world. There is a whole other world out there, and we are a part of it. We have to learn about it."

In 2006, he noticed it was an Olympic year, though not for the Summer Games. But his passion and patriotism sharing a healthy balance, Vendt was ready to represent his country and wear the flag again—on his swim warmup.

"The Winter Olympics were going on, and I heard that Olympic theme song," Vendt said. "Man, I knew I was coming back. I realized my career was definitely not over."

"The addition of Kaitlin Sandeno and Erik Vendt make it more fun," Phelps said. "It's more interesting to have those two come in and give us new flavor. Vendt, I can't wait until we go head-to-head in sets when he gets back into shape. People who don't know swimming don't know Erik and I went 1-2 in Athens [in the 400m IM]. I love that guy, and I'm excited he's here."

Vendt said training with Phelps was one of the reasons he liked Club Wolverine.

"He's so good in the water, you take whatever he has to say with a lot of importance," Vendt said. "His kicks off the wall, the technique—things you don't think about, you see him do it and think about it."

Teammate Davis Tarwater, another national team member, said the addition of both Bowman and Phelps boosted the program.

"I've adapted very well to his training regimen," Tarwater said of Bowman's training. "In fact, my whole experience with Bob has been very favorable. Obviously he's a very different personality than Jon Urbanchek, but Bob is also a great communicator and great coach. I truly enjoy swimming for him, and think we've helped him to adapt to the college environment, and it's a transition he's made unbelievably well. The second thing is having Michael Phelps here helps tremendously. It's really great because everyone has a positive outlook and is trying to achieve similar goals. To have a situation like this is very conducive to success because everyone's goal is to succeed—no one provides a negative atmosphere, so it's a very good group to train hard with."

Phelps said being around the college crowd helped him feel "normal." He said the experience was something he needed as a nineteen-year-old, and the rules and regulations of being on campus—

and swimming for Bowman—gave him a structure that most college-aged young men need.

"I hang out with a lot of the swimmers here on campus—I feel like a normal person," Phelps said. "Though there are a lot of restrictions, I am able to have fun and do what I want to do."

Phelps said having Jon Urbanchek, also an Olympic coach, around the program was also a boost.

"I love that guy—I think everybody does," Phelps said laughing. "He's always funny and out-going. His sly comments are always something that will make you smile. He's a one-of-a-kind guy. I really enjoy seeing him on our pool deck."

Phelps said he thought it would have been fun to be a college athlete, perhaps even in another sport besides swimming, though he admitted he was glad swimming was his bread and butter.

"In high school, I said I wanted to quit swimming and go out for the golf team, but I've still never really swung a golf club except on the driving range," Phelps said. "Swimming is the sport I love, and I can't go anywhere without it. So I'll stick with what I know."

His sister Whitney, who visited several times, said later that Michael's time in Michigan was critical to his social development and personal growth.

"He was forced to go grocery shopping, get himself up each morning, to the pool and to practice," Whitney said. "That made him grow up and mature, which he needed. Michigan is not that far away. We were always out there and when we were, we spoiled him like we did when he was little. I would bake brownies for him and we would all pitch in and clean and do his laundry."

For his outstanding performance in Athens, Phelps was named the 2004 United States Olympic Committee Sportsman of the Year. For the time being, though, Phelps was starting his academic life at the University of Michigan with a pair of classes, his first steps into academia.

His memories from public school aren't as, well, memorable. So starting school at Michigan was a big change.

"One of the things I'm actually excited about is going back to school. That's the first time in my life, really, that I've been excited to go to school and to continue that part of my life. This is an opportunity to start the second part of my life, and I'm going to take it."

Though he was not taking a full-time student schedule, he was looking forward to the academic setting.

"It's definitely different being back in class—it's good," Phelps said. "I'm just taking two classes to get back into the swing of things. I had to do my first real college assignment the other day, so hopefully that went well. It's definitely a new atmosphere, both in the classroom and in the pool. I'm getting used to training with a bunch of new guys, but things are going better than we thought. I had a meet a week ago. Bob and I predicted two seconds slower than I swam, so I guess things are on the right track. I'm just enjoying myself and getting back in the normal routine."

His first assignment was talking in front of a group of people in class, something he had been trained thoroughly at with microphones and tape recorders shoved in front of his face in Athens.

"It was a three-to-five minute speech just to sort of get to know everyone in the class," Phelps said. "It was college 'show and tell'—that's how the professor put it. We pretty much had to come in and bring something in, explain about it. One of my biggest things I've been proud of so far is winning an Olympic gold medal, and that's what I wanted to come in and talk about."

His speech was tight, and to the point—to the letter of the assignment.

"It was only three-to-five minutes, so [I] didn't want to get points deducted by going over," Phelps said. "My 2008 [Olympic] plans are, well, I'm back in the water right now."

And yes, he brought a gold medal to share with

the class. But only one—agent Peter Carlisle keeps the rest in a safe place. Which race was it from?

"I can't tell you. I can't read Greek. I saw '200m,' so it's 200 meters," Phelps said. "It's either the butterfly or the IM. They asked me, and I had no idea what it was."

Academics aside, Phelps was in Ann Arbor mainly to train and get better after nursing a lower back injury.

"I'm pretty much back to one hundred percent after being out of the water and having a small setback with my back," Phelps said. "One of the things Bob and I like is to be in a routine. If we're in a routine, things are good. I think getting back into the routine was something that was important to us. If I'm swimming and I'm going to school, then that's really all I'm doing. That's what I want to do. I'm ready to compete again. We had our goal meeting the other day to talk about things I want to accomplish this year, next year and years to come, so there are already goals that are set for the next four years, and we're starting to work for those."

Coach Bowman and Michael work together on all aspects of his training and racing. The two have changed the plan after most seasons, successful or not, and the season after the 2004 Olympics was no different.

"We're going to start swimming some new

events, I'll say that. We're going to open up some new doors and see where events take us," Phelps said about his strategy for World Championships in 2005. "One of the things I'm doing as a person is growing and starting to get some more muscle. Hopefully that will give me a little extra power that I didn't have last summer. Hopefully with that and being able to train up here with Peter Vanderkaay and Klete [Keller], some of those guys who are back in the water, hopefully all of us will be able to do something over the next year or two."

At the World Championships in 2005, Phelps swam well, again chasing the 200 freestyle gold medal, and this time coming away with it. Indeed, of the six events Michael raced, he was victorious in all but one: the 100 butterfly. He and Bowman went back to the drawing board, added an event to Michael's repertoire, and kept their eyes on Beijing.

His lead-up to 2008 was definitely on track after the 2007 World Championships. Phelps was coming off the best World Championships performance in history, winning seven gold medals. The "Worlds" are the equivalent of the Olympics in non-Olympic years.

Phelps' quest for eight medals at the 2007 Worlds, which were held in Melbourne, Australia, fell short when Ian Crocker jumped in too early on the preliminary heat of the last relay, the 4×100 medley. That resulted in the disqualification of the American team, so they weren't allowed to compete in the final for a medal of any color. Phelps set world records in winning the 200 freestyle, the 200 butterfly, the 200 and 400 IMs. Phelps and the rest of the 4×200 relay set a world record on the way to gold, and the 4×100 freestyle relay team with Phelps won gold with a World Championship record. Lochte knocked off Peirsol in the 200 backstroke with a world record for gold, but Peirsol won gold with a world record in the 100 backstroke. And Brendan Hansen avenged his 2004 Athens loss by beating Japan's Kosuke Kitajima in the 100 breaststroke. The United States dominated the 50 free, with Ben Wildman-Tobriner winning gold and "fastest man" in the pool title, and American teammate Cullen Jones took silver in the sprint.

Wildman-Tobriner was coming off a big 2007. While Phelps won seven golds at the 2007 World Championship, Ben was another who got a lot of attention for winning the 50 freestyle against the fastest field in history at Worlds.

"My goal was to final," he said of the 2007 gold medal at Worlds. "I mean, I didn't necessarily expect to win that title, if you want to call it that, but I knew I could potentially medal. So I exceeded expectations."

Before the Olympics, Wildman-Tobriner was finishing up his studies at Stanford and applying to medical school. In fact, in its coverage of the Beijing Olympics, the celebrity news TV show *Inside Edition* showed him working out shirtless, and called him a "real-life Dr. McDreamy."

"A real life Dr. McDreamy, huh?" Wildman-Tobriner wrote on Facebook after hearing about the show. "I'll have to try to get my hands on a copy."

Wildman-Tobriner admits he was shy as a child. He started out slow in swimming, and is not a fan of two-a-day swim workouts—called "doubles"—for children because it burns them out and causes swimming to dominate their lives. Ben was a lefty pitcher and first baseman in baseball, though he had to stop in middle school when he chose to pursue swimming at an elite level. Now, he can be seen strumming his guitar, which worked out well when he first got to Stanford and played music written by his roommate.

Though he is "book smart" to the highest degree, as a child, he was also artistically inclined in some ways, and as an elementary student made a picture frame and decorated it—inside it is a picture of little Ben in front of a mural he made with his class, and that picture still sits on his father's bureau.

He said his time at Stanford was not the academic cutthroat atmosphere that many top schools are thought to harbor. He said he liked hearing new ideas from a diverse crowd of bright people. He said it was not unusual for him to walk into his dorm and hear a concert pianist practicing, and remembers another student who worked for the Web browser company FireFox, and then Netscape. As a biochemistry major, Wildman-Tobriner liked studying medical device innovation, though he was unsure, even after medical school, whether he'd be a doctor or be a researcher and work in development.

While swimming is different from medical school, Ben said he expected that his swim training would help him in the future.

"First of all, it's nice to see hard work pay off," he said. "That gives you more motivation to train hard and do things you believe in. The translation as far as the skills go is that as you move from the pool to the real world, you know how to be calm under pressure, stay focused for a long period of time—characteristics that are helpful in the world in general, not only in medicine."

In a prophetic moment that would make Stanford proud, before the Olympics, Wildman-Tobriner said he was so impressed by Jason Lezak's "kick coming home," that he could not imagine someone catching Lezak in the final meters of a race.

While his parents no doubt take pride in his studies, they always put more emphasis on being a good person. At a Stanford event when Ben was an upperclassman, Ben had already made the U.S. National Team and was winning races everywhere he went collegiately. But at the school swim team event, the parent of a Stanford freshman swimmer pulled

Ben's dad aside and said that Ben had helped his son, and both he and the young man's mom were very grateful that Ben stepped in and gave their son some compassion and wisdom.

So the only blemish at the 2007 World Championships for the Americans was once again a relay—something that could haunt Phelps in Beijing, just as it had in Athens.

Phelps had matured as a swimmer and a thinker in the water. He knew he could not go flat-out every race—and would not unless he had to.

"For me over the past two years, to be able to swim the event program that I swam, I have been able to learn so much—to be able to manage my energy, both emotional and physical," Phelps said. "And I think in 2004, it was just every race I would go for it. I have been able to learn over the past two years to conserve and try to save up a little bit because my event program is so long."

Michael had some medical issues to deal with before the 2008 Olympics. He had bad lower back pain, and had to see a physical therapist to get treated for it. A source close to the situation said it was a stress fracture in the lower back, but because of privacy issues, no one would comment. Phelps also would not comment on the injury, knowing competitors see such information and use it for motivation or head games. He got his sister's respect, though, for fighting through it—she knows first-hand how hard back injuries are to deal with.

"I think a lot of swimmers go through physical therapy and have their pains and injuries. So it's sad when anyone goes through that. Michael works with great physical therapists, and has [a] great team around him who helped him get to where he is. Having the back thing like I had, [I] know what it's like to have that pain. It's frustrating and for him to continue to push through it, and go to physical therapy sessions, and to make his back, shoulders, and hips stronger, took a of work."

In October 2008, Phelps said he broke his wrist when he clumsily tried to enter his car in Ann Arbor, Michigan.

"I'm a fish out of water. I'm a clumsy person," Phelps told the Associated Press. "I fell and went to catch myself and I just tweaked it the wrong way."

He had surgery to insert a pin to speed the healing, and noted how 300 days out from the Olympics, while it was not an ideal situation, it would not hurt his preparations because he had time left to keep training.

However, several teammates from the University of Michigan said a more serious incident that happened about a year earlier put a bigger obstacle in Phelps' path at the time. In 2006, Phelps, who was of legal drinking age at the time, was at a party at a house near campus with other college students, including several teammates, where there was alcohol, certainly not uncommon for a college party anywhere.

All of his teammates interviewed about this 2006 incident said Phelps was drinking. Phelps was out on the porch of a house with the young woman he was seeing at the time, and a teammate. He got angry when someone's name he was not fond of was brought up in the conversation—though he was not angry at the people he was talking with—and punched a wooden pillar, wrapped in siding, with his fist, and broke his hand. His training had to be put on hold while the hand healed.

"I am 100-percent sure," a teammate who was there said in an email interviewing following a phone interview about the incident. "He punched the porch column, breaking his hand. This is the absolute truth. But that story never made it to the press."

The 2006 incident could have affected his preparation for the 2007 World Championships—where he would build the foundation even more for the run he was hoping for at Beijing in 2008.

"We were there at that party," another teammate said. "He got angry about something, punched it, and broke his hand. End of story."

Of course, this was nothing like the legal entanglement Phelps was in after his arrest and guilty plea for driving while impaired following the 2004 Olympics, which he served his community service for and it was wiped from his record.

Still, Phelps did nothing illegal, broke no laws— the only thing he broke was his hand. The former teammates, who asked not to be quoted by name because they do not want to be seen as criticizing Phelps because they don't want to "get in any trouble" with swimming officials or other coaches, said Phelps was a nice enough teammate most of the time, but was not in the social circle of the swimmers and student-athletes at Michigan. Michael lived in his own place and had friends from Baltimore who either lived with him or would visit him for periods of time. They said it was simply a case of Phelps being on a different track from the others there, who were "Michigan Men"—with the intent to graduate from the University of Michigan, whereas Phelps moved to Michigan to train at the University under Bowman, not pursue an academic degree. They all did enjoy video games. But when student-athletes and post-grad swimmers would gather and talk about academic majors, credit hours, internships and future jobs, and other school-related topics, it simply was not part of Phelps' program while he was there. After talking just a couple classes one semester and one class in another semester, Phelps did not pursue a degree.

The athletes said they did not hold that against him at all, and that he accomplished his goal of getting faster at Michigan – they all went to Michigan to create a better future for themselves, and that's what Phelps did, just without the school part. And while they spent little time, as a group and on average, with Phelps in social settings, he was a phenomenal training partner to watch in the pool at times, and knew the technique and training tools that could help them. Racing the very best, they said, made them all better swimmers.

Chapter 6

The "Thorpedo" on Swimming's Radar

Before anyone had heard of Michael Phelps, there was someone else who was supposed to equal or eclipse Mark Spitz's record of seven Olympic gold medals. In fact, when Australian Ian Thorpe won six gold medals at the 2001 World Championships, the prediction wasn't so much whether he would get seven gold medals, but how many times he might repeat that performance.

One must understand the unique spot swimming occupies in Australia. Along with Australian "football," swimming is the national sport, similar in status to professional football, baseball, or basketball in the United States. Swimming stars can write their own tickets, and the top echelon become icons and highly paid endorsers and celebrities in Australian culture.

Thorpe was ahead of Phelps in terms of developing as a teen. Just fifteen in 1998, Thorpe won a pair of gold medals at the World Championships, including the first of what would become many in the 400 freestyle. Thorpe hit a growth spurt, filling out size-seventeen shoes—almost literally flippers on his feet—and won four golds at the 1999 Pan-Pacific Championships. Thorpe had become the world record-holder in not just the 400 free, but also the 200 freestyle, an event he looked to dominate long into the future.

So the 2000 Sydney, Australia, Olympic Games, which figured to be Thorpe's hometown show, was at the start of a gold run that no one had seen since, well, Spitz. With his youthful exuberance—Thorpe was still just seventeen for the 2000 Games—Thorpe added the difficult 1500 freestyle to his arsenal of events, and promptly won the event in the 2000 New South Wales Championships.

But Thorpe still had not grown into those big feet, or those big expectations. While he was the star of the 2000 Games, he won just three golds, and just one of those came in an individual event, the 400 freestyle, in which he set a world record. Thorpe thrilled the home-country crowd in the 4×100 freestyle relay when he caught and passed American Gary Hall Jr. to deliver the gold home to the Aussie relay. Hall had talked about smashing the Aussies like guitars, so Thorpe and teammates mockingly played an air guitar celebrating the win, further endearing him to his faithful crowd and establishing himself as a kind of rock star in Australia.

However, in one of his signature events, the 200 freestyle, Thorpe faced the Netherlands' Pieter van den Hoogenband, who pulled away from Thorpe in the final and tied his own world record to win the gold medal ahead of Thorpe, who settled for silver. Worse, Thorpe went slower than he had in the qualifying heats, the first time that had happened to Thorpe. Though Thorpe picked up another relay gold, silvers in the 4×200 freestyle and the 4×100 medley relay left Thorpe with three golds and a pair of silvers, short of the five golds he had hoped to secure.

At the 2001 World Championships, Thorpe took off like the "Thorpedo" nickname he carried. He was literally unbeatable, as observed by a then-sixteen-year-old Michael Phelps, who was fresh off a fifth-place finish at the Sydney Games in the only event he had qualified in, the 200 butterfly. Fellow U.S. teammate, Tom Malchow, who, ironically, swam at Phelps' future home, the University of Michigan, had won the event in Sydney. Thorpe, however, was unreal, claiming gold in the 200, 400 and 800 freestyle individual events, and helped lead Australia to gold medals in all three relays as well. In all three of his individual events, Thorpe set world records, and contributed to another world record in the 4×200 freestyle relay.

Finally, in 2002, Thorpe had the quantity to go with his quality. He lit up the 2002 Commonwealth Games with six gold medals and a silver, the one "blemish" a second-place in the 100-meter backstroke. Thorpe stayed on track at the 2002 Pan-Pacific Championships, winning five golds—all three of his signature freestyle events, the 100, 200, and 400 freestyles—and gold on two of the three relays, with the only exception being the medley relay, as the Aussies did not have the dominant swimmer in each stroke needed for medley relay gold.

After Pan-Pacs, Thorpe's mental approach was questioned after he switched from his long-time coach to train with an assistant coach who had no international experience. Whatever changes he made in his program were not working. At the 2003 World Championships, Thorpe did win golds in the 200 freestyle and 400 freestyle events, though neither was an Australian, meet, or world record, and he slipped to a bronze in the 100 freestyle. In the 100 free, his time was among his better ever; however, the world's best had improved even more.

American Natalie Coughlin said Thorpe carried the weight of the swimming world on his shoulders for a long time.

"Ian Thorpe has been under so much pressure

for so long," she said. "I can't imagine how difficult it is for him. He's done a lot for the sport."

Leading into the 2004 Summer Olympics in Athens, Greece, Thorpe was part of the controversy at the Australian Olympic Trials, where he false-started in the 400 freestyle—in which he was the prohibitive Olympic gold medal favorite—and was disqualified. The man who qualified instead of Thorpe stepped aside to allow Thorpe to race amid allegations that Thorpe's spot in the race had been bought, and Thorpe went to Athens in the shadow of American Michael Phelps, who had no such coaching, motivation, consistency, or coaching issues and was on track to swim in eight events. In fact, Phelps even passed up potentially competing in the Olympics in the 100 backstroke, in which he was thought to be a medal contender.

In what was called the "Race of the Century" with van den Hoogenband and Phelps, Thorpe did win gold, van den Hoogenband silver, and Phelps bronze in the 200 freestyle, a race that Phelps was new to and was considered an outside chance for a medal. Thorpe emerged from Athens with golds in just the 200 freestyle and 400 freestyle, a silver in the 4×200 freestyle relay, and a bronze in the 100 freestyle—just four total medals, and only two gold medals.

Thorpe took "a break" from swimming, not entering the 2005 World Championships, but assured fans he would return to the Olympics in 2008, where American Phelps was supposed to give the Spitz standard another run. He tried to come back in 2006, dropping his signature event, the 400 freestyle, to focus on the 100 freestyle, against the advice of the Australian National Team coach. Thorpe ended up withdrawing from competition in 2006 from what was reported to be bronchitis, and moved to California to work with Coach Dave Salo. He went back to Australia in time for the 2007 World Championship Trials, but withdrew from trials and stunned Australia by announcing his retirement.

Thorpe, however, had become and remains one of Australia's top endorsers and celebrities. Though retired, he is on the payroll for his swimsuit sponsor, Adidas, and has deals with an airline and telecommunication company. An avid fan of fashion, he has done work for Armani and has his own line of undergarments and jewelry, and guest-starred on such American TV series as *Friends*, though just as an extra.

His opinion still matters to the swimming world, at least in Australia, and to the worldwide media who cover swimming. Just before the Beijing Games in 2008, he said Phelps would not match Mark Spitz's record of seven gold medals, much less surpass it.

"I have said before that I don't think he can do the eight, and still believe that," Thorpe told the London *Telegraph* as he arrived in Beijing. "Mind you, if there is any person on the planet who is capable, it is him. It's sad, but I just don't think it will happen."

While the media blew up the story as though it were Thorpe disrespecting Phelps—Coach Bowman gave the newspaper clipping to Phelps for motivation—Thorpe actually had more kind things to say about Phelps than negative, though the comment about Phelps not matching Spitz was what caught headline writers' attentions. He predicted that no matter whether Phelps matched Spitz that Phelps' effort in so many events was noteworthy simply for the undertaking itself.

"He is going to blow the world away, even if he doesn't achieve what he sets out to achieve," Thorpe said. "There are so many good swimmers out there. The standard is incredibly high. You've got to look at each of his individual races. He's up against incredible competition at the moment. Even some of his events that he has always been stronger in, like the 200 meters individual medley—that distance isn't there anymore," Thorpe said of the cushion between Phelps and his competitors in the past.

Perhaps Thorpe was even striking a compassionate tone for Phelps, knowing how the pressure of high expectations can crush a sporting soul, or how setting goals too high can mean anything but the highest level of accomplishment is failure.

"If he achieves, say, five gold medals, the world should salute that," Thorpe told the *Observer*. "He is one of the greatest athletes in the world. I just admire his tenacity in everything he does—in the pool, training out of the pool, in everything. He has set his targets and pursues them."

Phelps, however, was nothing but complimentary toward Thorpe.

"A lot of people look at him differently because of what he's done, but he's a normal person, and you can have a normal conversation with him," Phelps said. "All around, he's a good guy."

Chapter 7

Omaha, Nebraska: No Calm Before the Storm

While NBC was compiling footage of Phelps, and most people around the world expected to see him swim everything, there was still the little issue of the 2008 Olympic Trials to get through before the boxes could be checked to line up Michael Phelps for five individual events and three relays in Beijing.

Omaha, Nebraska, hosted the 2008 U.S. Olympic Trials, and after a tornado warning, fans were set to see a real storm unfold in the pool as some favorites bowed out—some after setting records—and some little-known names were about to secure roster spots.

Athletes and coaches talk about "taper" a lot at Olympic Trials. During the course of the swim season, the workload and training time begins relatively lightly, then plateaus. To prepare for the focus meet of the season, the coach lowers the workload gradually. This is the taper, and it usually takes anywhere from two weeks for longer distance swimmers to up to eight weeks for sprinters.

For example, most swimmers do between nine and twelve in-water sessions a week, and four or five out-of-water or "dry land" workouts per week. The swim practices at the beginning of the season are usually no more than four thousand meters and consist of a great deal of long, easy swimming just to get the athlete back into shape after he or she has had some time off (about two weeks). During the plateau part of the season, many coaches give out eight thousand meter practices a few times a week with more long, fast work in it where a high heart rate is sustained. At the end of the season, in "full taper," the athlete drops down to doing workouts of two thousand meters or less, focusing on details like sprints, starts, and turns.

The swimmer's body reacts to this by physically peaking. Swimmers in full taper are a sight to behold. For the seven or eight months of the nine-month training season, swimmers appear tired and wet and smell like bleach to the outside world. When a taper "hits," and the rest begins to accrue, swimmers start to smile. The workouts that have leveled them for months are starting to back off, and they have energy. They tend to get very hyper and can have a hard time keeping that energy in check.

Getting the timing of the taper right is arguably the most challenging part of a coach's job. Each athlete is different. Phelps really only needed the four weeks between the Olympic Trials and the Olympics to be ready for his best performances and world records at every turn.

"The biggest thing for us coaches is when you taper swimmers for a meet, it is like a haircut—you never know if it is any good or not until it is too late," Bowman said. "So once you have a few swims in, you can relax a little bit. It is before the not-knowing. I think it is the anticipation that is tough because it really is a leap of faith to some degree."

The goal of every taper is to get the athlete to drop his or her best times. If your best time is the world record, like Phelps, then anytime you do a personal best, you are setting the world record.

While some would miss their taper and not make the team, while others would peak at Trials and fade at the Olympics—Phelps had no such worries. Coach Bob Bowman was not about to let his competitors nationally and internationally know how beat-up or rested Phelps' body was at Trials.

"Taper, what does that mean?" Bowman said. "Obviously you prepare for this meet because it is so competitive. You can't just treat it like a normal meet. I would say that we are kind of at the end of a cycle of preparation and we are now going to start a new phase that goes into the Olympic Games, and

I feel like that while we came in here really ready, that we could have done some more things to have him better which is nice to know at this point."

His greatest competition for individual medley events was Ryan Lochte, who would also compete in the 200 backstroke where he would have to face at Trials, and in the Olympics, world-record–holding Aaron Peirsol.

"I think both of us hate to lose," Phelps said. "And you know I think one of the things that motivated me when I saw, I think Ryan had an article not too far back saying, I don't really know exactly what it was quoting but it was saying that when some people get in and race myself and Aaron, they are racing to get second—and he is not—and I think that fired me up a little bit. You know, like I said, we both hate to lose. I said this before and I will say it a thousand more times, he is a great competitor and a great friend."

Some swimmers set records, and didn't make the team at all, or at least in their event. Cullen Jones set an American record in the preliminary heats of the 50 free, and then failed to finish among the top two in the event, and thus didn't qualify to swim the sprint in Beijing.

"It is a deep field of talent," said sprinter Ben Wildman-Tobriner. "It's a plus and a minus. It's a great group, but it's hard to qualify for a U.S. team. Hey, you could be the defending world champ and not make the team. Nothing is given in any sense of the word."

Hayley McGregory, who came into the Trials ranked second in the nation, set a world record in the 100 backstroke prelims, but then finished a heart-breaking third in both the 100 backstroke and 200 backstroke finals, failing to qualify for the team in either event by one spot.

Gary Hall Jr., reigning gold medalist in the 50 freestyle, also failed to make the team. Neither Amanda Weir nor Carly Piper, 2004 Olympians, made the team. Brendan Hansen, the world-record holder at one time and multi-time reigning champion in both breaststrokes, did win the 100 breaststroke, but finished fourth in the 200 breaststroke, failing to qualify in that event. Yet that event had its own story of triumph, as Eric Shanteau, Hansen's training partner, was suffering from cancer—he'd put off treatment until after the Olympics—and made the team in that event.

With the Olympics—and thus Olympic Trials—only once every four years, everyone knew what was at stake, but it didn't lessen the pressure for anyone.

"It is an Olympic year—everyone prepares themselves for Olympic years," Phelps said. "I think everyone tries to compete for an Olympic year. You get that experience once every four years. You have World Championships every other year (years ending in odd numbers). You have Nationals every year.

81

But this is the Olympic Games. You get the chance to really go out there and represent your country and I think everyone is trying to prepare themselves the best way they can."

Omaha provided everything but a dull moment. Dara Torres, at age forty-one and two years after having a baby, qualified in two events plus a relay, though she planned to do just one event and the relay in Beijing. Torres was set to become a five-time Olympian and did not swim in 2004 after retiring following the 2000 Sydney Olympics.

"Dara, I've been calling her my mom," Phelps said. "At forty-one, with a kid, it's extremely impressive to have her come out here and win the 100 free tonight. It's going to be fun to watch. She was on my first Olympic trip."

Elder statesman Erik Vendt, who had been to two Olympics and had briefly retired to backpack around Europe and contemplated a career change after the 2004 Games, also made the team.

"Erik is . . . I'm speechless," Phelps said. "I remember when he first came back [to Michigan] and he absolutely destroyed everyone in the pool. We had been training, training, training, and he just destroyed us in a long course freestyle set. It was just shocking. The kid is amazing. I've never seen him more excited, more fired up than he is right now. He's looking forward to the mile tomorrow and hopefully he'll be able to put up a good time."

While the swimsuits were getting a lot of attention, Bowman pointed out that a lot of the swimmers setting records were people like Phelps, Peirsol, Coughlin, and Torres—all of whom had previously held records in the events.

"I think that this Olympics and even the last one, because you have people like Michael and Aaron Peirsol staying in the sport longer, they are able to stay at their peak level longer," Bowman said. "What you used to have was a new crop of people coming up and they would sort of have a breakthrough and maybe break a world record. Well, for these guys it is just doing their best times, and since they are in the sport longer, I just think that there are going to be more world records because the world record-holders are still in the sport longer."

Phelps would not predict what he would do in Beijing and if he'd be able to set world records.

"I am going to prepare for that meet just like I do every other meet," Phelps said. "There is only so much I can do in a month and then I am going to prepare myself the best that I can. If I step up onto the block and say to myself that I have done everything that I can, and that is all I can really tell you."

Reflecting on when he found out he had broken a bone in his wrist, Phelps flashed back to the initial feeling when the doctor told him. What, he wondered, did this mean to his Olympic quest, and all the preparation that had gone into the nearly four past years?

"I can remember when I found out that my wrist was broken—I was just devastated," Phelps said. "I had no idea really how things were going to come off of it. The timing really wasn't the best timing. You know I was just kind of like, I just sort of gave everything away, and I was negative for a little bit, but then after I was able to get back into the water right away. The only thing I could have done at that point was to stay as positive as I could because what had happened, happened, and there was nothing I could do to change that."

With his wrist and back problems pretty much in the past, Phelps was happy to look ahead to brighter months. One of his favorite teammates, Vendt, was being sued by swimsuit sponsor TYR for allegedly violating his endorsement contract.

"With the ups and downs we have had this year . . . it has definitely been a rocky year," Phelps said. "Good times and bad, but it has been fun and I am very satisfied with where we are now. With everything that has happened this year, the ups and downs, I am just happy to be doing my best times and I am having fun while I am doing it. I am racing hard and this is the best part. This is the thing I love the most, I love to race and that is what excites me the most."

After having the pressure of chasing Spitz in 2004, the questions were nothing new, and having that Athens experience helped Phelps mentally, too, with his approach.

"I think having gone through everything I went through from 2003 to 2004 leading up to the Olympics and really being thrown into the spotlight, not really knowing how to take it, not knowing really how to handle it, just go for it and have fun," Phelps said. "You know, having all of that happen, going through the last four years and leading up to this point, I think I am more relaxed now than I was four years ago. I mean, that is good for me. I think the more relaxed I am, the better I am so that is just going to be fun for me to step up to the Olympic level and wear the Stars and Stripes."

Phelps was able to talk to Mark Spitz at Olympic Trials, something everyone was hoping to see.

"In the awards area he was wishing me good luck and that is pretty much all he said," Phelps said. "He did say that if he swam two events back to back like that he would be in a coma. Ryan and I got a little kick out of that. I said this a thousand times, he is one of the greatest Olympians out there so you know having his support is pretty special."

Though few took note, toward the end of the press conference, Phelps said he thought the 400 freestyle relay would be hotly contested, and he even named the country who he expected the biggest challenge from.

"Our relays, I think, are going to be a big key," Phelps said. "I think the French 400 free relay is going to be a challenge and I think it is something we are looking forward to. I think the medley and the 800 free, the same thing. I think there are going to be a lot of countries out there who are going to step up because it is an Olympic year and try to put together four guys in a fast relay. Hopefully we can be the best and fastest team ever, definitely the fastest team ever."

Chapter 8

Mark Spitz: Michael, Watch Out in the 100 Butterfly

At the 1972 Olympics in Munich, Germany, Mark Spitz became the standard-bearer for Olympic greatness with seven gold medals, setting records in all four individual events he swam, freestyle and the butterfly—he did not swim the individual medley which requires breaststroke and backstroke—and all three relays.

As an eighteen-year-old in 1968—just a year younger than Michael Phelps would be for the 2004 Olympics in Athens—Spitz had predicted he'd take home six gold medals. Things didn't go according to plan, and Spitz won a pair of relay golds, and finished second to teammate Doug Russell in the 100 butterfly—whom Spitz had beaten in ten previous head-to-head 100 fly matchups—losing by half a second. That loss to Russell also cost Spitz a chance at a third gold medal on the 4×100 medley relay, because Russell won the 100 fly and thus earned the spot on the medley relay.

But 1972 was all Mark Spitz.

The Munich Games were also the site of the unthinkable slaughter of Israeli athletes. Spitz had already finished competing when eleven Israelis were kidnapped and murdered by Palestinian terrorists at the Games. Spitz was Jewish, and was evacuated as he could have been a target of the kidnappers as well.

But in the water, Spitz was nothing but golden.

Before the 2008 Olympics, Spitz was the featured guest at a press conference in Omaha during Olympic Trials in early July—more than a month before the Games in China would begin—to talk about Michael Phelps' pursuit of Spitz's record. Spitz said that while Phelps had improved, so had all of the other swimmers in his events, both from America and around the world.

"He certainly has more experience, but so does the competition swimming against him," Spitz said. "I would say that based on the experience he gained trying to do it four years ago . . . I would say that he has a great chance of doing it."

Spitz said Phelps had a "better chance" to win seven in 2008 because Phelps had come through with six in 2004, while Spitz had struggled to two gold medals at the 1968 Games in Mexico City.

"I would speculate based on what I know about how to win seven gold medals, so I would say that I am pretty accurate in this regard," Spitz said. "The fact that he is experienced, and in some ways more experienced than I was going into it because he won six gold medals and I only won two of the Olympics before I won seven, I think he is personally swimming through these trials as I did, not fully tapered."

Spitz could tell at Olympic Trials that Phelps was not tapered. A taper in swimming is where a swimmer is properly rested and trained to go their fastest times. After his first race at the 2008 Olympic Trials in Omaha, Phelps looked tired. Many of his competitors were tapered and "shaved," meaning they had freshly shaved their body hair to reduce drag in the water. Phelps had done neither.

"When he was telling the press that the first race was really hard, that is not what you really want to hear from someone swimming so many races on the first day," Spitz said. "That to me was a dead giveaway that he is not fully rested, but he is also smart enough to know that he does not want to let his competitors beat him, or even have the notion that he can be beat. So he is using this meet, as I did, as the ultimate taper. If you have been tapered totally for this meet, you would be a little flat a month from now. There is not enough time to get back into a sequence. It takes about six to eight weeks to really get back and he knows that, so I would suspect, I would expect that you are going to see him win by margins and set times that have never been done before, and he'll, he'll be unbelievable. That is what I suspect is going to happen."

Even though a lot was being made of Speedo's revolutionary suit, Spitz joked that Phelps would go fast in anything.

"I said this sort of tongue-in-cheek that if that suit had hair on it, Michael would set world records in it and everyone else would get in the same type of suit," Spitz said. "When I broke my first world record—and four the first four of my life—I wore two swimming suits. So I don't really think it's the swimming suit. If it was the suit, then I am going out and buying Tiger Woods' golf clubs because it means it does not matter who the swinger is, I am going to be able to score like that."

While the suit was getting a lot of attention for the world records, Spitz pointed out that swimmers had been setting records regularly at an alarming clip since 2000 as the U.S. and the Australians pushed the sport to the next level and the rest of the world hurried to follow suit.

"I think they would have been set anyway," Spitz said. "I mean the year before the Olympics and then the Olympic year is a time when somebody says to themselves, 'I am not going to have another shot at this and I am really going to focus . . .

therefore I really need to focus on the fact that I cannot stop fooling myself; I have to really concentrate on putting in an honest workout, taper properly and be rested and watch what I eat and my health because I am starting to get closer to the time when the Olympics are approaching and I want to be the best that I can and I want to start a year ahead of time.' So I think this is just a natural progression that, I think if you chart swimming it's not like box scores in baseball, but I think if you look back and chart the history of when world records are broken it escalates about a year before the Games and the year of the Games."

Though Ryan Lochte and Ian Crocker, and a host of other freestyle, IM, and butterfly specialists were close to Phelps' time, Spitz said that was a good thing.

"You can't win a race unless there is someone else in the pool with you—otherwise it is considered an exhibition," Spitz said. "Those people push Michael's greatness. On any given day, I always felt that I could have been beaten if I was not really concentrating on my game. So, I think that personally, those in the race with Michael certainly didn't wake up with a low expectation of themselves. I think they all have the same attitude that they want to win. And I also think that in some certain circumstances in some events that he will swim in, that if Michael doesn't focus and stay focused, he could be beaten."

Ironically, someone who, in his blog for the *Los Angeles Times*, predicted that Phelps would be beaten, Gary Hall, Jr., had a relative who pushed Spitz.

"Who pushed me? Well, when I regained the world record in that 200-meter butterfly I did it by a hundredth of a second and that was against Gary Hall, as in Gary Hall Senior, not Junior," Spitz said. "He was always right there. I had a guy by the name of Jerry Heidenreich that was right on top of me in the freestyle events."

Spitz said that swimming so many events does take a toll physically, but the bigger cost extracted is mental.

"It is not difficult [physically] for Michael and it was not difficult for me because we trained for it but I think it is to stay focused," Spitz said. "I honestly once or twice was walking out in a trance, to go swim in the finals of the Olympics I was going, 'Is this the 100 fly or is this the 200 free?' I mean of course I knew what it was because all I had to do was look up at the board and notice it was the 200 freestyle because I could see that was what it was. It's funny because as strange as it may seem, when you wake up in the morning, your training and your warm-up is all predicated on what you do ceremonially in that race."

The challenge for Phelps, Spitz was certain, was to keep everything together mentally from the start of his first race until the wall was touched for his last race. Any sort of lapse, no matter how temporary, could knock his plans off track at any juncture of the Games.

"I think that it is difficult to stay focused for eight days," Spitz said. "It got a little easier because for me every race that I won was an event that I never had to swim again for the rest of my life. So I really felt like they were taking bricks off of my back and the load was getting easier. I think that Michael will think the same thing as each day gets a little easier as each day goes by. I personally think that he is not thinking about seven gold medals. He is taking one day at a time. He is going to be honest with himself, he is going to say, 'I want to swim the best race of my life. I have never been better in my life. I am focused and I am tapered and everything is working well, and I may never get a chance to swim in this event again, who knows, and I want to go out with the best race that I can swim that day.' And over six or seven or eight days you are going to see that happen and he will come away with something that will be phenomenal."

Spitz admitted he could relate to Michael in ways many others could not.

"I see the tremendous similarity inasmuch as that his experience in going from one Olympics to the next, that he has won commandingly in the events that he is now going to participate in over the rest of the world," Spitz said. "It is quite difficult to imagine that one of his competitors is going to think that on any given day now going forward that it is going to be his day, because in the past five times they have gotten up and been beaten by him. Even in light of the fact you not only do your best time and break his old world record, you are still looking at his feet. I think that is a little demoralizing. To think that things could change four weeks from now is unlikely, and I would think that is what Michael is thinking also."

Many thought Phelps would try to do too much at the Olympics. But at the level Phelps is at, Spitz said as long as the events are manageable, building up some momentum could work in Phelps' favor.

"Because when Michael wakes up in the morning [at the Olympics], he is going to take each day one day at a time," Spitz said. "He has got to say to himself, 'My very first event I start rested like the other seven I am going to compete against in the 400 IM.' And like when I swam my first event, the 200-meter butterfly, I said, 'This is a great way to start and to prove to myself that I had rested properly, that I have tapered properly, and that I am ready to go.' And of course he has an additional seven more events that he can enter to prove that once he gets into his winning ways, that those who sit around on day number four or day number five who only have one event will start to second-guess themselves—whether or not they have rested properly, or whether they have tapered properly, and whether or not they are ready to go. It makes it really difficult for his competitors to think that they can stop this momentum."

Spitz did point out that he was speaking from the perspective of someone who had been there, and done it himself. So to imagine there were no obstacles was ridiculous.

"I am not a betting man and I am not going to wager a bet in Las Vegas on this," Spitz said. "But if I had to handicap his chances of winning his events, I see three different areas that he would run up against as a difficulty. One is the very first event because you need to obviously get off with a win on the very first event, and the 400 IM is quite an arduous race to say the least. I would say that he has no control of the relays or what will happen. He'll only participate as one of the members so there is always the risk of someone false-starting or the team that tries to place them in the finals maybe does not get there. You don't know how well the other countries are going to respond to swimming relays because anything can happen."

Spitz's greatest race of concern for Phelps was the 100-meter butterfly, which had several up-and-coming international stars, many of whom swam for American colleges, along with American Olympic teammate Ian Crocker, the world record holder.

"The third thing is whether or not he, in the only event he does not hold the world record—the 100-

meter butterfly—can continue his winning ways," Spitz said. "I think at the [2007] Worlds he won by hundredths of a second. And I watched him win by one one-hundreth of a second when I was there in Athens [2004], and if you know that is the way you have to win a gold medal, and it is well into his program, that probably may be one of his most physical races that he will have to swim to be able to accomplish what he wants to do. And if I think back on my career, I also had a race that was of a similar nature; my most physical race was the 100-meter freestyle. I am sure that he thinks about that. At least I would if I was him, but I am not."

Spitz said whether Michael equaled or surpassed Spitz's totals, he just hoped he enjoyed and savored it.

"I think this is a marvelous time for Michael Phelps," Spitz said. "I am hoping that he embraces this opportunity and relishes it because I know that I personally did that when I went to Munich. And I really felt comfortable and confident that I was going to have my day because of the results that I was able to achieve at the Olympic Trials. I think it is marvelous for him, I think it is great for the sport of swimming, and it is certainly great for the Olympic movement, and NBC has got to thank him immensely because he is their meal ticket for the first week of competition."

Kidding aside, Spitz said he'd be glad if the company he kept included someone like Phelps.

"All that being said, I think it is about time that someone else takes the responsibility and I am happy to pass the baton on to somebody that I know, that I am sure that I have inspired," Spitz said. "There is nothing bad about that—it is only positive. So, in one sense I am saying to myself, 'Hey, it's okay, records are made to be broken including mine.' Thirty-six years is a long time. I would have never thought that I would be sitting here if someone could have said, 'What do you think you will be doing in the year 2008?' As a matter of fact it just dawned on me that it was forty years ago that I was at training camp, and I was going, 'Wow, that is almost twice as old as Michael Phelps is now. Wow, I swam a long time ago.'"

If Phelps hadn't yet won over Spitz by 2004, he did at the Athens Olympics. With virtually no shot at beating Ian Thorpe and a host of others in the 200 freestyle—an event Phelps had just added to try something new and expand his event list—Spitz was impressed at the courage that took. Phelps knew he probably would not win, but also knew that he would be better for it, something Spitz admired.

"When I think about Michael not only swimming events that he not only holds the world record in but also challenging himself in events that he is the second-fastest or third-fastest in the world and putting them into his program and that is more than I did," Spitz said. "I think it is grand that he does that, and because he does that I think one of his greatest races to date was getting third in the 200 freestyle in the 2004 Olympic Games in Athens. That is why he is the world record holder in that event now. That is why he will win that event in Beijing. That is why now he is even more capable of winning seven or eight gold medals. You cannot take that away from him, and it does not take anything away from me. So that is the way I feel about it."

Phelps was making millions of dollars a year swimming before the 2008 Games. When Spitz was at his peak, professional swimmers could not make a living, not just because the money was not there, but because they had to be amateur athletes at that time. That was part of the reason Spitz retired in 1972 after his seven-medal haul in Munich, at just age twenty-two, because he wanted to accept the financial opportunities that his fame brought him, which meant he gave up amateur status. Now, swimmers can go professional as teens and still be Olympic swimmers, though they forsake their collegiate eligibility, which Phelps, Katie Hoff, and Kate Ziegler have done. So would Spitz have continued to the Montreal Olympic Games in 1976—and possibly more medals, perhaps even a repeat performance—if it were financially viable, and profitable?

"Seven gold medals, um, seemed to be a nice time to hang my suit up," Spitz said. "But had I had the opportunity as you put it to be able to continue in my sport and make money like the athletes are able to do today, then it would have certainly been in my best interest on behalf of my sponsors to continue in the sport. Certainly I would have gone to Montreal and at that point in time I would have only been twenty-six years old, but I am convinced that I would not have probably attempted to swim that many events. I think I would have drawn back to the events that relatively would have seemed easy for me which probably would have been the butterfly events because those are the ones that I had won by the greatest margin. I probably would have swum some of the freestyle events to qualify myself for relays and may or may not have elected to actually bow out of the individual events."

That being said, Spitz does not resent a dime of what Phelps has earned, and it warms Spitz's own heart to know that he paved the way for Phelps, and lots of others, to make a living doing the sport they, and he, love.

"It is good for the sport that they have been able to make money so they can stay in it," Spitz said. "Had the rules been the same today as they were yesterday for me, I don't think Michael would be swimming now because I think he would have taken the money opportunities that were showered on him from his success in Athens—he would have been categorically denied to continue in his sport from that point. The money has been grateful and gracious to him, and we have been able to watch him swim and this is going to be history. He is going to do what we say is, 'A little schooling,' to the rest of the world and it is going to be exciting to those who will see it in person and for those who will watch it on TV."

Should be exciting. Indeed.

Chapter 9

What Could Go Wrong?

While the focus was on what Michael Phelps would have to do in order to even think about seven gold medals, much less eight, a lot less focus was on what could go wrong. In fact, in the era of only-the-best-is-worth-reporting and number-one-at-all-costs philosophies in the media, reporters and fans alike only looked at the times Phelps had posted the past eighteen months to point to why he might be able to do it. Of course, that was assuming he could equal his best effort in every race in every single Olympic event. What they didn't consider was what could go wrong, and there were far more variables, some out of Phelps' control, that could prevent him from even coming close to repeating what he had done in Athens, much less what he was being counted on to do by sponsors, the media, fans, and USA Swimming at the 2008 Olympics.

Every recent Olympics, a gold medal–worthy swimmer from the United States has come down with a mysterious stomach bug. Whether it's from the water, local cuisine, or an illness, it has dashed more than a few medal hopes. Natalie Coughlin, the female American with the highest hopes for a swimming medal haul in Beijing, is a prime example. It was Coughlin who had her entire year of hard work wiped out at the 2005 World Championship when she fell ill suddenly the day the competition began. In the off-Olympic years, Worlds serve as de facto Olympics and are the focus of the year. To fall ill there was a crushing blow to the U.S. medal tally. In 2004 in Athens, American Ian Crocker, who had then and has now the Olympic record in one of Phelps' events, the 100 butterfly, had a stomach bug that slowed him down. Even in Beijing, Ryan Lochte, the closest thing to Phelps in the swimming world—and one of Phelps' teammates—was sickened and weakened for a couple of days by an intestinal illness.

Phelps' primary rival on the team in terms of multiple events was Ryan Lochte, who could probably have had his own five or six gold-medal shot if not for Phelps.

"It's nice to know people are starting to compare me with Michael Phelps and everything," Lochte said. "But as far as people saying, 'You and Michael have to race,' I don't care about that. It doesn't get in my head."

Lochte said having Phelps as a teammate in 2004 inspired him.

"Because every time he stepped up, he laid it all on the line, didn't hold anything back—he was like that every time," Lochte said. "And to go back-to-back like he kept doing was awesome."

Phelps would have to dodge illness, something he had little control over, especially in the tight quarters with teammate Lochte, who swam several of the same events.

Another adjustment came with the timing of the events in Beijing. For the first time ever, finals would be staged in the morning to allow for late-night, nearly live, prime-time broadcasts in the United States. All swimmers' entire international careers had been shaped around swimming a prelim in the morning, getting a nap and some nutrition, and coming back in the evening ready to race a semifinal or battle for a medal. Now, he would have to wake up ready to roll in his highest gear. That certainly was the case for all swimmers in China, but no one could guess who would adjust well to the new format, and who would have a hard time resetting their body clock, workout regimen, and focus.

With times faster than they have been in the history of the sport with the new, buoyant swimsuits and a commitment to improvement by such nations as China, France, Germany, and Japan, America and Australia would no longer be the only ones contending for podium finishes. Some of the best U.S. college swimmers were from foreign countries, and didn't have to go through the grinder that is American Olympic Trials, where only the top two U.S. swimmers qualify for each individual event. Even world record holders, like Hayley McGregory, and former gold medalists fell short of making the U.S. Olympic Team, sometimes by mere hundredths of a second. Rather, the foreign exchange students had to only be the best two in their own country, allowing them to basically coast at their own Olympic Trials (if they were even held) and set their training to be perfectly tapered for Beijing.

Rowdy Gaines, the former U.S. Olympic star-turned-NBC commentator, told me right before Olympic Trials that not only would the Trials eliminate several of the sport's top stars, but would "hobble those who left it all in the water" at the Trials. With their best performances in Omaha, some would drag their tired bodies to Beijing where they would not even approach their best times.

"It has happened to a lot of athletes, especially those just trying to make the Olympic Team, that they make it and then have nothing left—physically most have something left, but mentally, they left it in the pool at Trials," Gaines said.

Phelps being a favorite at Trials was something that would bring an amount of pressure, Gaines said. Almost no one could understand what it is to be under its crushing weight—Gaines had been a favorite in 1984, and admitted he "folded under the pressure" of Olympic Trials.

"There's nothing worse than being a favorite at the Olympic Trials. I wouldn't wish that on my worst enemy," Gaines said. "No question about it; literally, no question about it. I'm not lying. Trials were more pressure than I have felt in my swimming career, in my life. There's nothing even close."

Not only would Phelps have to be at the top of his game at the Trials, but he would also have to be prepared to shine at the Games, and so would his relay teammates, not just the three he swam with in the finals. To even make the finals, four other swimmers would swim in the preliminaries, where only the top eight countries would advance to the finals. Any single swimmer having a bad day, off on their taper, or battling an illness could keep the relay from advancing to the final. Another possibility was a disqualification, which had happened as recently as 2007 at the World Championships in Australia, where Ian Crocker false-started, thus disqualifying the relay—and America had to re-qualify for its spot right after that at the U.S.-Australia Duel in the Pool. Without that final opportunity, and without turning in a best time, the United States would not even have qualified to be in the final relay at the Olympics, leaving Phelps to go for, at best, seven medals.

Someone rising up and pulling out the best swim

they had ever done is not unheard of at the Olympics. There is a very real possibility that virtual unknowns can become household names, like Mary Lou Retton, Rulon Gardner, and the 1980 "Miracle on Ice" Olympic Hockey team. Factor in that hundredths of seconds separate the winners from losers in several events, and others are decided by tenths of seconds, and Phelps' margin for error, every time he went for a medal, would be zero, literally less than razor thin. Even teammates like Crocker and Lochte had been seeded ahead of Phelps in events at various times.

Swimmer Michael Phelps before his first Olympics in 2000.

(© Duomo/Corbis)

Another record: Phelps sets a world record in the 400 individual medley during the "Duel in the Pool" in Indiana in 2003, which pitted swimming powers the United States and Australia against each other in a head-to-head matchup. *(©Donald Miralle/Getty Images)*

Phelps reacts to missing the world record in the 100 butterfly at the 2003 "Duel in the Pool"with Australia.

The torch is passed: Phelps (top) leads U.S. teammate and former record-holder Tom Malchow in the 200 butterfly final at the 2003 World Championships in Barcelona, Spain.

In Barcelona, Spain, at the 2003 World Championships, Phelps celebrates winning gold in the 200 fly.

(©Shaun Botterill/Getty Images)

Phelps starts off in the semifinals of the 200 individual medley at the 2004 Olympic Trials in Long Beach, California. *(©Al Bello/Getty Images)*

From left: Bronze medalist Phelps, gold medalist Ian Thorpe of Australia, and silver medalist Pieter van den Hoogenband after the 200 freestyle "Race of the Century" at the 2004 Athens Olympics.

(©Sipkin/dailynewspix.com)

Phelps dives in during a race at Canham Natatorium at the University of Michigan in November, 2005. Phelps trained in Ann Arbor, Michigan, from 2004 to 2008.   *(©Tony Ding/Icon SMI)*

Phelps at the Kodak Theatre in Los Angeles for ESPN's 2007 ESPY Awards.

*(©Michael Germana/Globe
    Photos, Inc.)*

Whitney, Debbie, and Hilary Phelps listen to the national anthem following the gold medal presentation after Phelps' 200 butterfly win in Beijing.

(©Jason Reed/Reuters/Corbis)

Phelps celebrates after winning the gold medal in the men's 4 x 100 free relay final at the Beijing Olympics, Aug. 17, 2008.

(©AP Images/Luca Bruno)

Ricky Berens and Ryan Lochte join Phelps in cheering home 200 free relay anchor Peter Vanderkaay in Beijing, Aug. 17, 2008.

(©David McIntyre/Black Star)

From left: Phelps, Brendan Hansen, Jason Lezak, and Aaron Peirsol of the United States pose with their 4 x 100 medley relay gold medals at the Beijing Olympics, Aug. 17, 2008.   *(©Reuters/David Gray)*

Whitney, Michael, their mother Debbie, and Hilary
on the NBC *Today Show* in Beijing, Aug. 18, 2008.

(©*Kristian Dowling/Getty Images*)

Chapter 10

China Takes World's Center Stage

Though some on the 2008 U.S. Olympic team were not old enough to remember, China was not always known as the world's dominant Communist super-power.

Before splintering into several countries, the Soviet Union was a force in the Olympics, and used what were considered to be professional athletes—who were paid to play their sport—long before professionals were allowed in the Olympics. East Germany had also been a major player in the Olympics through the twentieth century until Communism largely came to an end, with the primary exceptions being China, North Korea, and Cuba.

China has developed a modern economy, and indeed become a major economic player in the world of business. China has become a global power to be reckoned with, and with the largest population in the world and a growing economy, it figures to be among the countries needing the most resources, including oil, in the future.

Human rights conditions are widely regarded as lacking in China. Freedom of speech is not guaranteed, and the practice of free speech often lands citizens in prisons. All that being said, China is one of the world's oldest civilizations, going back more than six thousand years. Ancient China is credited with such inventions as paper, the compass, gunpowder, and printing. A cave not far from Beijing has human fossils that could date back as far as a half-million years ago, though it's more likely closer to two hundred fifty thousand years ago, according to various scientists.

The last and most recent Chinese civil war pitted the People's Republic of China (PRC), made up most significantly of mainland China and Hong Kong, against the Republic of China (ROC), which controls four islands, most notably Taiwan. The end of the civil war was particularly hard on mainland China. Only the death of previous hard-line Communist leaders allowed for economic development that, starting around 1990, pushed China onto the world's stage as an economic superpower. The PRC, however, still deals quickly with anyone who speaks out or is otherwise deemed a threat to the political, social, and economic conditions there. The PRC is seen as a socialist state led by a "democratic dictatorship." The islands governed by the Republic of China have a multi-party "representative democracy."

Beijing is the capital of the PRC, though it is not the largest city—Shanghai holds that title. But Beijing is recognizable to anyone who saw it in pictures or movies from decades ago, because it still has the remarkably preserved luxurious palaces, temples, and stone walls.

Of course, nothing is more familiar to outsiders than the Great Wall of China, which runs for nearly four thousand miles. Such "great walls" were built in China as far back as 600 B.C. to protect against invading enemies, connecting fortresses, though many of the original walls have since eroded.

The current Great Wall was built during the famed Ming Dynasty after the Chinese had failed to defeat Mongolian and Manchurian tribes. The Ming decided the best way to deal with the nomadic tribes was to build great walls along China's northern border. The Ming capital, now known as Beijing, was an area with a particularly well-fortified area of Great Wall. Beijing was known as Peking well into the twentieth century. Peking means "northern capital," following a tradition in east Asia of naming cities that incorporate location and capital status. For example, the city of Nanjing, China, means "southern capital." The Japanese city of Tokyo means "eastern capital."

But to the current generation and those thereafter, the city will be known by its current name of Beijing. With so many people, Beijing needs an incredibly giant and comprehensive transportation structure to move people around. The city has the country's largest rail system, and the two largest of those stations have more than three hundred thirty trains coming and going daily. Beijing is also connected outward to the rest of the country by nine expressways, with six more major, functional thoroughfares. However, with just eight underground rail lines, the city's seventeen million citizens often have to use different modes of transportation. In contrast, New York City's eight million residents have twenty-six underground rail lines.

Such limited mass transit options are what, along with a high-density population, contribute to the poor, even dangerous, air quality in Beijing.

The city is filled with historical buildings and areas. Tiananmen, which means the "Gateway of Heavenly Peace," was built during the Ming Dynasty in 1420, and is considered the entrance to the Imperial City, which is home to the famed Forbidden City.

Tiananmen is contained by the gargantuan Tiananmen Square, which was constructed in the mid-1600s. It was expanded to four times its original size and completed with cement in 1958, and has since become a focal point for a lot of attention, both positive and negative, in China. The Proclamation of the People's Republic of China was made in the Square by Mao Zedong on October 1, 1949. Protests in 1989 resulted in the unforgettable image of a lone Chinese man standing in front of a tank, blocking its path. Those protests led to massacres that, by Chinese Red Cross estimates, left two thousand six hundred dead, though the Chinese government said the total of dead was less than two hundred fifty. NATO's estimate was later released claiming six thousand died.

But in 2008, the modern city of Beijing, if not the rest of the country, was opened to the world to host the Olympic Games.

Less than two months before 9/11, Beijing beat out five other countries—Malaysia, Cuba, Spain, Egypt, and Thailand—who bid to host the Games; the International Olympic Committee chose China on July 13, 2001.

The previous Summer Games, in 2004, held in Athens, Greece, were marred by construction delays, cost overruns, and fears of terrorism attacks planned for the Olympics. Though no terror events had occurred outside of the Olympics since the Munich massacre in 1972 of Israeli athletes—the year Jewish-American swimmer Mark Spitz won seven swimming gold medals—Athens was on high alert. It should be noted that the 1996 Olympic Games did have a fatality during a domestic bombing by a former

U.S. Army soldier and anti-abortion activist, which is, by definition, terrorism.

But in Athens, the convergence of such forces— union unrest, terrorism—pushed several venues' completion past deadlines. In fact the pool was so far behind schedule that plans to roof it were scrapped, though the open-air facility in Athens was eventually largely praised.

In China, labor strife and terror are largely non-issues, and in a Communist state, civil unrest and foreigners hoping to conduct terror activities are dealt with swiftly and harshly. In fact, even Internet users in China are not allowed to visit sites viewed as subversive to the government. Protestors hoped to seize upon the Communist country's dismal civil rights record, and to drum up public outcry world-wide to change conditions in Tibet. While the occasional protest drew media coverage, it was pretty obvious the efforts were not well organized or allowed to make the logistical planning for such efforts to be effective.

The structure that housed swimming, the "Water Cube," was an aesthetic gem, and construction was final in January 2008, well in advance of the Games. The rectangular building was the brainchild of Australian architects, Chinese engineers, and Chinese designers. It was the Sydney-based, swimming-obsessed Aussies who came up with the familiar "bubbles" covering the Cube. Using one hundred thousand square meters of ethylene tetrafluoroeth-ylene, "air pillows" on both the inside and outside give the appearance of air bubbles, and allow more natural light to enter the building than traditional glass. As many as nine hours a day, the pool is lit by natural light.

The pool itself was designed to create the best conditions for world records. It was one meter—more than three feet—deeper than standard interna-tional pools, which allowed for fewer waves, which, in turn, provided less wave disturbance for swim-mers during races.

Part II

Chapter 11

Beijing 2008: Saturday, August 9

The opening day of swimming went as Phelps had hoped. His schedule, as planned by himself and Bowman, was laid out nicely, with only the preliminaries of the 400 individual medley. Michael blazed through his heat with the best time of any of the four heats at 4:07.82, with only one other swimmer breaking 4:10.

The 400 was one of the two longest events on Phelps' Olympic docket. The pool is fifty meters long, so for a 400-meter race, it is down and back four times. The individual medley includes all four strokes, two laps of each—the butterfly, backstroke, breaststroke, and freestyle.

Ironically, Phelps would have to count on his teammates as much as himself to win three of those medals—the ones from relays. One of the keys would be thirty-two-year-old sprinter Jason Lezak, who would anchor the first and last relays of the Games.

The way Jason Lezak tells it, he is good at one thing. Going fast, and in one direction. A straight line.

Lezak's first job was delivering pizzas. He got lost—a lot. The elder statesman of the U.S. Olympic swim team points out that that career was before cell phones, so he had to figure it out on his own, or stop and ask for help. Of course, all of the getting lost didn't help with tips.

Then again, Lezak already knew what he was good at in life. In school, he had no interest in spending hours on particular classes. He liked math, because he was good at it, and it came to him relatively easily compared to other subjects. There wasn't a lot of reading to it, just crunching the numbers, and coming up with a total.

In China, that's all Lezak would have to worry about, being at least an eyeblink faster on the two key relays to keep Michael Phelps' golden dream afloat. Go faster than the guy next to you. Math, at its simplest. Except when the race was extrapolated to include the facts that the guys he was going against were the fastest in the world in that distance—the 100 freestyle. And that he'd have the weight of the world, the weight of Phelps' hopes, the weight of the U.S. Olympic team, on his shoulders.

Still, it was just about the math. Go faster than the guy next to you.

After being criticized by teammate Gary Hall Jr., in 2000 and 2004—Hall did not end up making the 2008 team—Lezak had refocused himself. Getting up in the morning after the disappointments, and the ensuing criticism, from the 2000 and 2004 Olympics was tough on Lezak. He had to read or see broadcast comments about how he was not good in the clutch, how if a big swim was needed and the top podium spot was on the line, Jason Lezak might not be the best choice to bring home the coveted hardware.

"I think about the future, forget about the present, and worry about what my goals are," Lezak said. "So each morning when I wake up to go to the pool, after debating for a few minutes, I realize what the important things are, so I get up and go after it."

Lezak's Olympic dream was born in his home of Los Angeles, when in 1980, he was able to go watch the Olympics.

"That was the first time I was able to go to the Olympics, to see them in person. I was just blown away by it," Lezak said.

The 2004 Olympics had not been kind to Lezak. He failed to advance to the finals in the 100 freestyle in Athens in 2004.

"I had a lot on my table, with the 100 and 50 and the relays. I made a mistake for saving myself [in the qualifying heat of the 100 free]—of giving my best effort in the right places," Lezak said. "So it was also a learning experience. It's not about being a perfectionist. It was a big mistake I made. That's happened at smaller meets, but I thought it could never happen at the Olympics. It did. So, yes, I learned from it and would do it differently if I had the chance again."

In Athens, the American 400 free relay fell apart, though Lezak swam the fastest leg of the relay.

"Things could have gone better in the prelims of the 100 and then the 400 freestyle relay, too," Lezak remembers.

That 2004 Athens Olympics 400 freestyle relay won bronze, but had it delivered the gold it was expected to, Phelps would have had his seventh gold medal, and would have tied Mark Spitz right then and there for most golds in one Olympics. Hall had swum on the prelims of that final. Hall also won gold in the 50 free, an event contested nationally by him and Lezak for several years until a fresh crop of sprinters emerged after 2004.

Lezak had briefly pondered retirement after 2004, mainly because of the negativity, and even doubts he had about himself. But knowing there was more out there, he could not turn his back on a final run.

Even in an interview as late as 2005, Lezak was not certain 2008 was something he would stick around for.

"Right now, it's year to year," Lezak said. "I have dedicated myself to swim this year, 2005. I have no intention of retiring. So it's one year at a time for now. Maybe in 2006, I will decide to work toward '08, but for now, it is year by year. I still think I can do better. I will know in my heart when the time comes not to do this anymore, but I don't have that feeling yet. I enjoy it as much as ever. It's one of those things like life in general, where if you are happy doing what you are doing, you usually do well, whether it's school, work, or anything."

Lezak knew if he didn't win gold in 2008, that while the initial disappointment would sting—perhaps more than ever—that no matter the outcome, he'd still be better off for the decade-plus career as a professional athlete. He remains unsure if he'll continue swimming when he finally retires.

"That's one of those things I will look at when I'm done—I have had so many friends who have retired who still swim to keep in shape," Lezak said. "But this sport has taught me a lot, made me in a lot of ways who I am as a person. It's taught me responsibility, time management, and even how to be a good business person. So it's been the best experience I could have asked for, especially the discipline."

Something else that keeps Lezak going is the fan base he has built. At the end of big meets, even if he hasn't done as well as he had hoped, the young fans calling his name and clamoring for his autograph continue to buoy his spirits.

"It's one of those things where I used to be one of those kids—I know exactly how it is for them," Lezak said. "So for me to be on the other side in that situation is still a remarkable thing to me every time. I feel pretty lucky to even have people looking up to me. It's important to me to be a good role model and to always try to do the right thing."

Lezak's personal life had taken a satisfying turn as he decided whether to keep swimming or retire. He married Danielle DeAlva, an Olympic swimmer for Mexico. So when he went home after a frustrating meet or just got tired of the sport, he had someone who not only loved him, but could relate to what he was going through, and offer honest assessment and encouragement.

"Ever since I met her, and ever since we were married, I've been as happy as I've ever been," Lezak said. "Regardless of any setback in the pool, I am happy, because that is secondary to my wife, who is the most important thing to me. Since she was a swimmer herself, she can relate to what I'm feeling or going through. Swimming is so different than any other sport that the average person can't understand what we go through. But this is great. She supports me one hundred percent."

Danielle, who was studying at the time to be a

nurse, had a lot to do with healing her husband's emotional wounds.

"She's a great teammate," Lezak said with a smile. "It's so nice to have someone who has your back all the time, and getting over some things from the [2004] Olympics really helped me recover. It's funny because she supports me, and I support her. She took some time to figure out what she wanted to do, whereas I've been swimming for nine years. So it's been a great deal for both of us. I'm very fortunate."

Yet in the same breath, Lezak pointedly said that if he did have success in 2008—whether that meant just making the Olympic team at Trials or medaling at the Olympics—that it would be attributed to the disappointment he suffered through.

"Definitely [the adversity] shaped me, because you have to learn from it and come back stronger," Lezak said. "That was the thing about 2004 in Athens. The Olympic level is probably a hundred times harder than the World Championship level, so it's not something you recover from overnight. Talking about it helped a lot. And I did realize there is a lot more to life than Olympic medals, but at the same time, it pushes me to do better next time. I'm looking forward to that challenge."

Even though he didn't hit his goals, Lezak knew every morning when he woke up that he was living a dream he was unsure existed when he started swimming.

"I didn't even know [being a professional swimmer] existed back when I was in college, to be honest with you," Lezak said. "I thought that college was it, and you were done. When I finished college, I didn't know there was such a thing as a professional athlete in swimming. After I won a national title, someone said, 'You might get a contract.' I asked, 'What do you mean?' So to be able to swim professionally for nine years is incredible. I look at guys like Matt Biondi and Tom Jager who had to quit swimming in their prime, when they could have improved even more had they continued. But the way it's evolved nowadays with endorsements, swimmers can continue and try to go faster and faster for much longer than those who paved the way and came before us."

The 2007 World Championships were a surprising learning experience for Lezak. It was more than a final test run for his Olympic push to 2008. He knew he had to prove, just one year before the Beijing Games, that he had the right program, mental and physical, to not suffer through another experience like Athens in 2004.

"I think [2007 Worlds] was a good learning experience for me," Lezak said. "I didn't want to make the same mistakes I made at the Olympics or other meets where I saved myself up. I was first after prelims and semis this time, and while coming in fifth was tough, it's a good step for me to go three hard races in a row, which gives me room to improve."

However, 2007 World Championships also produced an equally important revelation—and concern for Lezak and even Hall: The U.S. sprinting ranks had all kinds of new talent after years of just Lezak and Hall being constants. Ben Wildman-Tobriner, Cullen Jones, and Garrett Weber-Gale had gone faster at times than Lezak in the 50, and Jones and Weber-Gale looked like they'd contend for 100 freestyle spots. Only the top two finishers at Olympic Trials in each event compete in those individual events at races—even though the top six go on the relay team—so Lezak had more than his work cut out for him just to make the team. But Lezak actually looked at it positively, and welcomed finally being pushed to go faster.

"I still think there could be a lot more improvement in our 100 [freestyle], but the fifty guys are really moving," Lezak said. "And guys like Cullen can go fast in both the 50 and 100, so it's good to see good people doing so well. You always still try to win every race, but when a teammate is a good guy and beats you, it feels a little better. That being said, I'm still out to win, just like they are."

While so much else was going on in the sport—the new swimsuits, the domestic and international rivalries, the Chinese political landscape and their Olympic hosting issues—Lezak said his plate was full enough simply focusing on Olympic Trials.

"To tell you the truth, I'm just focused on the Olympics and making the team," Lezak said. "The Games could be anywhere, and I'd be excited. I just have unfinished business to take care of. That's not to take anything away from China, because there is a lot of excitement as there should be, and from everything we hear, China is putting together a great Games."

As the 2008 Olympic Trials approached, Lezak had pronounced this his time.

"This time I'm not just trying to get a spot—I want to go in the 50 and 100 [freestyles], and both relays," Lezak said. "So I will go in with more confidence."

Leading up to the 2008 Olympic Trials in Omaha, Nebraska, Lezak said he was to the point of taking offense to the question "Can you beat him?", whether it was about Hall or another competitor. Lezak, who had as a child gone trick-or-treating as the Grim Reaper, had his own skeletons to dispose of in China. He'd have not one, but two, chances early in the game to keep Phelps' quest alive as soon as it had begun, and if all went well, at the end of the Games, in the final relay.

Lezak also paused and sighed before answering the familiar "Will you retire?" question, this time regarding whether or not he made the 2008 Olympic team.

"Here's the thing: Right now I'm really enjoying

swimming, and I love to compete," Lezak said. "It will get to a point where that's not the case, where I don't want to be doing this anymore. But that time is not now. I am focused only on next year, and I can't make any predictions past that. I'm motivated now in large part from things I didn't accomplish in 2004, things I want to accomplish. I'm my harshest critic. I see myself go through ups and downs and not always being on the victory stand, and when it all comes down to it, you have to always be yourself. There's no façade. I'm just me, for better or worse."

Though it appeared that two of the three—Wildman-Tobriner, Jones and Weber-Gale, and even perhaps Hall—would take the only two spots in the 50 freestyle at the Olympic Trials, Lezak shrugged it off. He said he could make "better memories" in the 100 freestyle.

"With my galloping stroke, I am probably best suited in that regard for the hundred," Lezak said. "Not getting air in the fifty, I miss a little of my power—they are two different strokes for me."

And what about his chances once he gets to Beijing?

"You have to be focused and ready to roll," Lezak said. "And trust me, I'll be ready."

Chapter 12

Sunday, August 10: Finals, 400 IM

Phelps started the Olympics with the 400 IM. The finals were Sunday, August 10, just after 10 a.m. The Olympics' biggest star didn't wait to shine the brightest. Phelps took down the world record with a time of 4:03.84.

"I'm not downplaying this race by any means, but I have to put that race behind me," Phelps said. "I have to act like it never happened because I have so many tough races ahead of me."

Phelps was more than two seconds ahead of second-place Laszlo Cseh of Hungary at 4:06.16, whose father was an Olympian in 1968 and 1972, also Mark Spitz's two Olympics. American Ryan Lochte took the bronze at 4:08.09, after being slowed by a stomach illness.

"I knew I was going to need a strong breaststroke

when we all turned together at the wall," Phelps said. "Ryan turned dead even with me, so I knew I was going to have to overpower him in the breaststroke."

Lochte said Phelps didn't take his bait to sprint at the start.

"I guess you can say I went out too fast, but I knew I had to get out fast," Lochte said. "The backstroke took a lot out of me, but I did my best. I can't ask for more. Michael competed the whole way and did really well. He had a great race, and I'm really proud of him."

President Bush was on hand to watch.

"I told Bob [Bowman] that this would be my last 400 IM, so I wanted to go out there and get a good time," Phelps said. And a world record by two seconds definitely qualified as a good time. "Afterwards, I looked up and saw President Bush giving me a thumbs-up and holding the American flag. That was pretty cool."

Just an hour and ten minutes after that were the semifinals of the 100 breaststroke, an event that Phelps debatably could have added and would have had a chance at qualifying in at Trials, especially had he focused on improving that event. But the schedule would have been prohibitive, and he would have needed to make the top eight to final. There is a chance Phelps will look at a breaststroke even for London in 2012.

Besides, it wasn't as if Michael had nothing else

to do that day. That evening he had to come back and swim the prelims for the 200m freestyle, a race he added just before the 2004 Olympics, where he went on to win a bronze medal in the event. On this night Phelps was second in the eighth of eight heats, going 1:46.48.

Chapter 13

Monday, August 11: Finals, 4 × 100 Relay

This was a busy day. At 10:19 a.m., Phelps had the semifinals of the 200 freestyle. Knowing he had to leave something in his energy tank but still qualify, he loped in with only the fourth fastest time for the finals at 1:46.28, with teammate Peter Vanderkaay winning their heat and becoming the top seed for the finals at 1:45.76.

Phelps had to turn around just one hour later at 11:27 a.m. and swim a 100-meter leg of the 400-meter relay, and though he's fast by any standards, he has never competed internationally in the individual 100-meter freestyle because he has not shown himself to be a pure sprinter.

A lot had happened outside the pool regarding the 4 × 100 free. The United States had two first-time

Olympians on the final relay, Cullen Jones and Garrett Weber-Gale.

Weber-Gale was a relative unknown in his first Olympics, though he had won Nationals, done well at Olympic Trials and had previous international experience. He swims at the University of Texas, which trains with the Longhorn Aquatics, the professional version of the college team that included Peirsol, Crocker and Hansen.

After thinking he might be a basketball player, Weber-Gale was only five feet tall in eighth grade and realized he wasn't going to have a future in that sport. He actually enjoyed playing dodge ball and basketball more with kids in his neighborhood in his native Wisconsin. Catch Weber-Gale on the slopes, and he's a terror on a snowboard or skis, though he had to stop both to train for college and Olympic swimming. Weber-Gale also painfully admits that he always wanted to be Zack from the teen TV show in the early 1990s, *Saved by the Bell*.

Weber-Gale has long appreciated being on national teams.

"The thing is, we weren't UT, Auburn or Cal or USC—we were representing the USA," he said after the 2005 World Championships in Montreal. "I hadn't thought about how different it would be cheering for the USA, but it was so much different. It's such a bigger thing than a college team; instead of a 'sub group' of people, this was representing a nation."

What surprised Weber-Gale in the post 9/11 world is that the U.S. athletes were not subject to the international resentment that other youth teams experienced since the United States went to war with Iraq.

"There are, to be sure, a lot of different views about the U.S. from other countries," Weber-Gale said. "But we just went out there and represented our country the best way we could—by being respectful and caring, and by doing our best. That was one of the things I thought going in—that there's going to be tension between certain countries and the United States, or between Israel and countries from the Middle East, but it wasn't like that at all. This is the amazing thing about sports, that it didn't involve other aspects—it was a 'pure venue.' We weren't competing for land or politics, but to just do our best, see who could go the fastest, and be good people. That's all we were trying to do—not show political views or anything. This gave me a different view of the world—there doesn't have to be so much negative going on, that's what I took from this."

Weber-Gale said being around the veteran swimmers on international teams helps the younger swimmers develop the confidence, attitude and preparation skills they need to be successful.

"That's something really important," he said, "to be able to learn from these older guys—just how to do what might seem like little things that really are big, like representing our country in a respectful way, how to get ready for races, and how to deal with fans—those are things that make a huge difference so you have to learn."

Weber-Gale learned that being a leader is shown by how one acts, not what they necessarily say.

"They led by example, not by telling you what to do or making big speeches at team meetings, but with their mannerisms and how they carried themselves, how they gave T-shirts and autographs to little kids, and dealt with the crowd," he said. "Some kids were coming up to me asking me for my autograph—and in my mind I'm not a big-time swimmer, but I carried myself the same way."

Neil Walker, a former Texas swimmer who stayed and trained with Longhorn Aquatics, is one of Weber-Gale's role models.

"I was a wide-eyed kid with him at one time," Weber-Gale said. "That made me realize how cool it was to see these little kids asking for my autograph. This lady in the crowd said, 'You must hate giving all these autographs.' I said, 'No way, I enjoy it.' And I enjoyed getting autographs from swimmers when I was younger. I told this lady, 'Some day in ten years, these kids are going to be doing what I'm doing—signing autographs for excited kids; I love it.' So it was just an unreal experience."

Not making the Olympic team at the 2004

Olympic Trials really gave Garrett a focus he needed in 2008 to avoid the mistakes he made four years earlier.

"I have this quote from [UT assistant] Kris Kubik," Weber-Gale said. "I was just totally broken up at the time, bawling. Kris came up and said, 'The way to get through this is to take a minute, remember how this feels, and don't ever let it happen again. Then every day in practice, work so that this doesn't happen again.' I promised myself that day I wouldn't feel that again—that much disappointment. It's important, to me, to keep promises to myself—it's a big deal. So when I compete, I mix in a love for racing with all the things that have happened in my past, people doubting me or that experience at the Olympic Trials, and it helps fuel me; when I get ticked off I go even harder."

He got some words of wisdom from someone in his family after missing the 2004 Olympic team.

"It's been a long road for me, after not making the Olympic team," Garrett said. "My grandpa, who I have always listed as a great inspiration, told me that hardships along the way are great, because once something good happens you'll appreciate it more and deal with it better."

Jones, who had won the 50 and looked like a lock to make the team in two individual events, the 50 free and 100 free, had missed on both accounts at the

Olympic Trials, qualifying only to swim on the relay. Cullen Jones has not taken the typical path to stardom as a swimmer.

The Bronx, New York City, native was five years old when he nearly drowned at a water park.

"You know," Jones said with a smile, "I didn't start off as this child prodigy in the water."

But he did learn to swim. He started entering races, but no one could have predicted in the early 1990s when he started racing how far he'd go in the sport.

"I was the one getting the purple or pink ribbon, the kid in lane seven going slow," Jones said. "So it is nice to have all the hard work I've done through the years paying off, but I still remember what it was like not to be fast. So I'll stay as humble as possible."

Jones didn't start swimming until he was eight years old, so he certainly did not start as young as many elite swimmers did.

"I played basketball for a while, actually for a good chunk of my life," Jones said. "I started swimming at age eight. Also, I did gymnastics when I was younger, probably started when I was six or seven, and I feel that helped me a lot with swimming—with flip turns especially. Because when the coaches taught me flip turns at swim practice, they didn't have to teach me twice because I had learned how to flip in gymnastics, and that really helped."

Once he took to the water, however, he never wanted to get out of the pool.

"I loved being in the water, and I was always passionate about it," Jones said. "My passion for swimming has only increased, too, the past few years. As a kid I was definitely that pool rat that you couldn't get out of the water. I stopped playing basketball in high school—I didn't go out for the team—because I wanted to focus on swimming. I also played water polo in high school, and if I ever stop swimming I'd probably go play water polo."

While he does all right in the deep end of the pool now, he's also a deep thinker. He majored in English and studied psychology in college at North Carolina State.

Losing his father when Jones was in high school shook him to his core. He remains thankful to have a strong mother as well.

"My dad passed away when I was sixteen from lung cancer. It was so sudden; one day he was healthy and the next day he was sick and dying—it happened fast, even though he did fight it with a lot of determination. He was smart as a whip," Jones said. "The thing I can say about him is that he really didn't want me to swim in the beginning. He wanted me to stay with basketball. He had been this amazing basketball player and because of things out of his control he had to stop playing. But once he saw swimming was what I wanted to do, he was one hundred percent behind me—even when he and I knew I wasn't any good at it. He would sacrifice all the time—selling something he had or going without to, say, buy me new goggles. As for my mother, she's a huge role model. People would always ask us after my father died, 'How can you two be so strong?' She's just a strong woman, and also very determined. I'm so proud to be her son."

Jones became the first African-American to set or be part of a relay world record. He also broke the American record in the 50 free, thus becoming the "fastest American on earth" as the winner of the shortest sprint is known, at the 2008 Olympic Trials when he went 21.59 seconds.

"I am not afraid to talk about it at all," Jones said. "The only problem is that my story might be a little boring. I mean, I didn't have this huge event where the sky parted over a pool one day, and I suddenly said, 'That's what I'm going to do.' I love being in the water, and I love to swim. I started out slow, worked really hard with my coaches and team-mates, and got faster."

However, in the finals at the 2008 Olympic Trials, he wasn't as fast, and not only did not make the Olympic team in the 50 freestyle—just the top two do—he lost his record to teammate Garrett Weber-Gale, who went 21.47 seconds. But Jones made the Olympic team as a relay member in the 100 freestyle.

Jones would be counted on like never before on the second day of finals at the Olympics for the 400 freestyle relay if Phelps was going to go eight-for-eight in gold medals. A black swimmer would help his white teammate make history—the only thing standing in their way would be a group of countries that wanted nothing to do with the red, white and blue.

The American relay team members that swam prelims—Nathan Adrian, Jones, Ben Wildman-Tobriner and Matt Grevers—had gone a world record time of 3:12.23 in prelims.

Matt Grevers made his name as a 100 backstroker, something he would win a silver medal in individually behind Peirsol in at the 2008 Games. But he was a strong enough 100 freestyler to make the 4×100 free relay as well. In fact, before the Olympic Trials, Grevers thought he was only going to make the team in the 100 freestyle—the top six, rather than two, who finish in the 100 freestyle make the U.S. team because of the relay, whereas only the top two make it in the 100 backstroke.

"The 100 backstroke is loaded with Aaron Peirsol, Randall Ball, Ryan Lochte and on and on," Grevers said. "Backstroke's a fun event, something I enjoy, but I'm not too confident with it in making a high-end U.S. team."

If only he knew then how things would turn out in Beijing.

Grevers, whose nickname is "Dutch," swam for a solid academic school, Northwestern, though it is not among the collegiate swimming powers. But he said the academic rigor of Northwestern fit him perfectly once he figured out as his freshman year went on how to manage his time. Grevers said he picked his college based on his academic interests.

"You can't swim forever," Grevers said. "Northwestern has a great degree [program], and I can go further in life graduating from a school like this. Plus I like the 'big fish in the small pond' aspect."

Though Grevers had also been a top 50 freestyler in college, once he saw the likes of Wildman-Tobriner, Cullen Jones and Garrett Weber-Gale, Grevers knew he had to shift his focus.

"For some reason, I haven't raced well in that," Grevers said of the 50 free. "Something always happens, and I just don't do well. Small things are so important in creating a 50, and I haven't hit the small things. If you mess up on the start or if you're past your stroke when you hit the wall, it doesn't happen. Guys like Cullen Jones and that fast group right now, they are so talented, so I leave that to those guys."

Grevers had made the lower-level teams, and though his progress was slow at times, it was consistent. He never had the big breakout swims that put all the eyes of the swimming world upon him— perhaps nothing that indicated an Olympic medal was within his reach—yet he had improved consistently, something he was proud of.

"I've been spending some time trying to rise up through the ranks, and it's been working out for me," Grevers said. "Hard work does pay off. I would love to be the poster child for progression. That would be an honor."

Grevers, who unlike a lot of swimmers doesn't follow the sport closely because he doesn't focus on how his competitors are doing because he'd rather work on his own improvement, said his parents encouraged him not to place limits on himself.

"They've always believed in my swimming and school," Grevers said. "They taught me to dream big, and I always have. My dreams are big, and my goals are always beyond my reach, but they believe in me. I might come up short, but that's what pushes me to do better, having big dreams and big goals, and working hard toward them."

So while he wanted to make the team in individual events—the 100 back and 100 free—he said before the Olympic Trials that the relay was his bigger goal.

"Even with the great sprinters we have now and have had in recent years, we haven't, as a country, won a lot of 400 free relays, and I want to help do better than ever in that event," Grevers said. "We have a young era of guys who will hopefully rise up and take that title back. To be a part of that is a dream of mine. It's not like we've swum badly in that event or the 100 free, I'd just like to be a part of us dominating again."

Though he admits that at six-foot-eight he often feels people stare at him for being so tall—he has concerns that it intimidates people at times. He doesn't envision himself as intimidating at all once people get to know him, and being tall helped get him into sports. He started in basketball, and seemed to have a bright future in it before going with swimming. But basketball did teach him how to play as part of a team.

"I had to choose at some point, and it was hard to, because I loved basketball. I like the team aspect," Grevers said. "That's why I like relays in swimming, because I like people counting on me."

The United States liked counting on Grevers, too.

In Beijing, the French had also used other swimmers for the prelims, qualifying second at 3:12.36 and setting a European record. The Australians qualified third for the final not far behind, with a time of 3:12.41. All three countries were below the previous world record time the U.S. put up in 2006, 3:12.46. It looked like a team might have to at least break 3:10 and set a world record to win the gold.

With his shark tattoo on his left hip, French star Alain Bernard, the world record holder in the 100 free, proclaimed before the race that France would have no problem beating the young Americans in the 4×100 relay. "The Americans? We're going to smash them. That's what we came here for," Bernard told the media. "If the relay goes according to plans, then we'll be on a roll."

This would set the tone for the Olympics and fire up Phelps like never before.

"Bob [Bowman] had said that the French team was saying some stuff, talking a little bit of trash," Phelps said. "It fired me up more than anything else. We were all fired up."

Still, the Americans looked like they were doomed in the race. None of the first three Americans—including Phelps, who went first and swam his leg in 47.51—broke 47 seconds. Cullen Jones had the third—and slowest—leg at 47.65, leaving 32-year-old American Jason Lezak trailing the world's fastest 100 freestyle sprinter, France's Alain Bernard, at the start of the final leg.

But Lezak turned in a relay performance for the ages—and the fastest of all time—at 46.06 seconds, catching and passing Bernard, who swam 46.73, and out-touched Bernard by eight one-hundredths of a second, 3:08.24 to 3:08.32. The Americans broke the world record Jones and three others had set the day before by just one-hundredth short of four full seconds to claim gold. Phelps was out of his mind with adrenaline, yelling loud enough to be heard a continent away and flexing his entire torso and upper body like he was in the Mr. Universe contest. The French, who Phelps congratulated individually on the medal stand in a show of sportsmanship, had to settle for second after watching their gold medal get virtually stolen away by the swim of a lifetime from Jason Lezak.

"Before the race, we all knew by the way the French had swum in the prelims that when they added their best two guys, it was going to be a tight race," Lezak said. "They had talked a lot about it, and we would just rather do it in the pool. I knew it was going to come down to the end, and I was hoping to be ahead when I dove in, but I never lost hope. I don't know how I was able to take it back that fast, because I've never been able to come anywhere near that for the last 50."

Lezak was on the losing end of this race as anchor at the last two Olympics, and that did cross his mind.

"I'm not going to lie," Lezak said. "When I flipped at the wall I thought, 'There's no way.' Then in the next instant, I was like 'No, this is the Olympics. I'm not giving up.' I got a super-charge and just took it from there. I can't even explain it, it was unreal. I've been a part of the two teams at the last two Olympics that came out behind, and I think I wanted it more than anybody, not just for myself, but to show that we are the nation to be beat in that relay."

Phelps appreciated Lezak's effort.

"It was unbelievable," Phelps said. "Jason finished the race better than we could have asked for. In the last 50 meters, I was like, 'This is going to be a really close race.' Jason in the last 50 was incredible. As you could see, I was pretty excited. I was very emotional."

Bernard would, days later, win the 100 freestyle individual event, with Lezak in third. But Lezak gave all he had, and a little more, to keep Phelps on track, and to get his relay teammates their own gold medals as well.

After some rest and several thousands of calories of fuel, Phelps was back that night, just after 7:30 p.m., for the preliminaries of the 200 butterfly. How he found the energy and focus is something only the likes of Phelps and Mark Spitz can understand. But after going back to the Athletes' Village for some rest and food, Phelps came back in the evening and won his heat with an Olympic record time of 1:53.70, while only two others were below 1:55.

Chapter 14

Tuesday, August 12: Finals, 200 Freestyle

At 10:16 a.m., Phelps had the 200 freestyle finals, the event he had taken a bronze in during the 2004 Olympics in Athens, losing to gold medalist Ian Thorpe, who was very much the Mark Spitz or Michael Phelps of Australia, though Thorpe never reached the heights many envisioned for the "Thorpedo." He was the best swimmer of his era, though, winning three golds and two silvers at the 2000 Olympics in his native Sydney, and at the 2004 Athens Games he took away two more golds, one silver and one bronze, and retired two years later, even though he had planned to retire after the 2008 Games. Thorpe was poolside in Beijing to watch Phelps swim, after predicting before the games began that Phelps would not win seven or eight gold medals.

In prime time for American viewers, Phelps broke the world record, going 1:42.96, winning by nearly two seconds in the 200 freestyle. Winning the silver was Taehwan Park of Korea. Peter Vanderkaay, Phelps' teammate from Club Wolverine at the University of Michigan, coached by Bob Bowman, claimed the bronze medal.

"I was lucky enough to get out in open water in the first 100, which is something Bob [Bowman] and I talked about," Phelps said. "I couldn't ask for anything else so far over my three races. I'm happy with the way things are going, and I'm happy with how [finals] went. It's a good sign for races to come."

The win earned Phelps his ninth career Olympic gold medal, which tied him for the most ever with Mark Spitz and track legend Carl Lewis.

"That's a pretty amazing accomplishment," Phelps said. "It's definitely an honor. I've been able to spend some time with Carl Lewis and exchanged a few words with Spitz here and there, so it's definitely pretty amazing."

Dealing with all the emotion that came with the dramatic relay win was a challenge for Phelps.

"It's not easy putting that behind you," Phelps said. "It was so emotional. But I had to force myself to put it out of my head. I have a lot of events ahead of me, and to be able to do what I want to do, I have to be one hundred percent focused."

Less than an hour after winning the 200 freestyle,

Phelps was back in the water for the 200 butterfly semifinals, where he needed to finish in the top eight to secure a spot for the finals.

The timeline would have been worse had Phelps stuck to his original plan—the 100 backstroke finals were less than an hour after the finals of the 200 freestyle. Less than three months earlier at the Santa Clara, California, Grand Prix, on May 18, 2008, Phelps faced Peirsol in the 100 backstroke—and beat him, a day when Phelps won both the 100 freestyle and 200 IM, winning all three events within a span of one hour. But doing the 100 backstroke in China would have been too much. And Peirsol won the gold—the silver went to Matt Grevers, who Phelps had also beaten that day in Santa Clara—so it was a one-two showing for Team USA.

Phelps had the rest of the day off, no doubt a much-needed break. The 4×200 freestyle relay qualifying heats were that evening, but the United States had young star University of Texas standouts David Walters and Ricky Berens, three-time-Olympian Klete Keller, and Phelps' Club Wolverine teammate, Erik Vendt, on hand to take care of business; they set an Olympic record in their preliminary heat.

Chapter 15

Wednesday, August 13: Finals, 200 Butterfly and 800 Free Relay (4 × 200)

At 10:21 a.m.—morning in China, prime time for most American viewers—Michael Phelps took on the world's best in the 200 butterfly. With his easy victory, he became the all-time world leader with his tenth Olympic gold medal.

Phelps won with a world record time of 1:52.03, and then took off his water-filled goggles and cap and looked disgusted with himself. He didn't pause at the moment to realize that he had just passed Olympic icons the likes of Mark Spitz and Carl Lewis for most-ever gold medals.

"My goggles kept filling up with water during the race," Phelps said. "I wanted 1:51 or better."

Goggles are obviously not supposed to fill with

water. Worse, it had happened right at the start when he dove in, so he swam four lengths of the pool against the best in the world hardly able to see. He still beat Hungarian Laszlo Cseh, who took the silver at 1:52.70.

"When my goggles did fill up, there was nothing I could do," Phelps said. "I knew there was no chance to clean them. I could just swim. That's the only thing I could do at that point. I couldn't take them off; I had two caps on. I couldn't rip them off. I couldn't fix them. I couldn't empty the water out. I just had to swim. I tried to see something. But the finish and the 150 wall, I couldn't see. I was trying to make it out. I was trying to see the 'T' on the bottom and try to time my turn and the finish, but I was more or less sort of counting strokes. I sort of know how many strokes I take per 50, and I was hoping that I was going to be getting on it and I was going to be able to hit the wall perfectly. I was able to get my hand on the wall first. It was a best time, but I think I was disappointed that I know I can go faster than that. It just disappoints me that my goggles— I did have a malfunction. There was nothing I can do. I handled the situation the best way I could."

Once again, the scene belonged to Phelps, who was declared the greatest of all time. In addition to Spitz and Lewis, Phelps' gold medal haul finally topped runner Paavo Nurmi, from Finland, and gymnast Larysa Latynina, who competed for the

Soviet Union before its split into a series of countries.

"I think I'm kind of at a loss for words," Phelps said. "Growing up, I always wanted to be an Olympian, and now to be the most decorated Olympian of all time, it just sounds weird saying it. I have absolutely nothing to say. I'm speechless." Phelps went on to describe the experience: "I think it started setting in a little after the butterfly. I kept trying to focus on my next race, but I just kept thinking, 'Wow. Greatest Olympian of all time.' It's a pretty cool title, I guess you could say. It's pretty neat. I'm definitely honored."

Ironically, under the plan as it had been written four years ago, Phelps would have been in the 200 backstroke later that night—he scratched the 200 backstroke right before the 2004 Olympics, where he had been scheduled to be in six individual events and three relays. He and Bowman realized that was too much for Athens, and backed the program down.

Phelps credited his coach for the accomplishments—and the well-thought-out program.

"I don't think I would be where I am today with any other coach," Phelps said. "From the intelligence—he's so intelligent in the sport, and he cares so much about every one of his athletes. He's very thorough. It's in every aspect. If I'm feeling the slightest bit injured or a pain or something, he says check it out. He's always on top of things. I'm fortunate enough to have a coach like him who is always there by my side through anything. We've been through a lot the last four years. He's still there and we're going to work together for the next four."

That's a good thing. Because in China, the thirteenth was not a lucky number for Phelps in terms of scheduling. One hour after the 200 butterfly finals, Phelps was in the water on the 4×200 freestyle relay. Phelps did the opening leg followed by Ryan Lochte, who was feeling well again, followed by Ricky Berens, and Phelps' Club Wolverine teammate, Peter Vanderkaay. The Americans were just too much for the world, winning in a world-record time of 6:58.56. Breaking the seven-minute barrier had been unthinkable to most in the swimming world; Russia took second and the silver medal an astounding five seconds back.

Athletes often speak about how they are competing for family members as much as they are for themselves. For Peter Vanderkaay, that took on a more literal meaning. At the 2008 Olympic Trials, Vanderkaay was joined by all three of his brothers, who also qualified for Trials. The oldest brother is Christian, Peter is next, Alex follows Peter chronologically and is a standout swimmer at the University of Michigan, as is the youngest, Dane.

Peter was the only one to make the Olympic

team, as he did in 2004, and was part of the gold-medal-winning 800 freestyle relay in Athens. In 2008, however, he had his staple events, the 200 and 400 freestyles—the 200 is what earned him another post on the 800 relay—and Peter also added the 1,500, the longest race in the Games.

An asthmatic since age ten, Peter is very reserved. He said his time in Athens did not change him, even though he came home a celebrity after heading to the Olympics a relative unknown, except locally.

"I don't think it's that much different," Peter said of life post-Athens. "I look at myself as the same person. Some people might look at me differently, but I haven't changed."

What didn't change was the academic tenacity Peter showed in the classroom, which is something his parents raised both Peter and his brothers to strive for—otherwise, they would not let their boys swim.

"I try to set high expectations for myself in and out of the pool," Vanderkaay said. "I know that swimming isn't a sport you can do forever. Some can make a career, but somewhere down the road you will need education. My parents always stressed it, and it is important to me. I bring the same expectation to swimming, too."

He was also seen, despite being a first-year Olympian, as a good leader and teammate, someone who earned respect from everyone who met him.

"I think it does go back to the way I was raised, some of the values of my family," Peter said. "That's always been important to me, to carry myself like that through all aspects of my life."

Taking schoolwork seriously was something that Peter said he enjoyed, because he did not want swimming to consume all of his waking hours and thoughts. But the work ethic he has in the classroom he also brings to the pool.

"I think it's just keeping your nose to the grindstone, and a balance—you have to have good balance in your life," he said. "I know a lot of other good swimmers talk about having that good balance. I keep school and swimming separated, though."

Peter said being outspoken does not always equate to being a good leader, and that having an internal confidence solves a lot of problems before they can start.

"I think it's more about focus than anything else," Peter said. "Confidence does play a large role in being successful in whatever you do. Being focused and ready for a race, or whatever it may be, is something that yes, is a key."

However, the unique Dutch name is often butchered at swim meets by announcers and telemarketers.

"I get sales calls asking for 'Vanderkee,'" Peter said. "They just totally mess it up. But it's not that hard to know how to spell."

While Peter enjoyed training with Phelps and Bowman, he said previous coaches and Olympians also added a lot to his development as a swimmer.

"I trained with some of the best guys in the country," Peter said. "I also trained with some of the best at Michigan—Klete [Keller] and Tom [Malchow]—so I learned a lot from them, too. I've been fortunate to have guys like that to look up to at Michigan."

While he reached the pinnacle—the Olympics—in 2004, he said it only told him one thing: that he was still far from reaching his potential.

"There's always room for improvement," Peter said.

That improvement, Vanderkaay said, comes from consistency, and being open to learning from others.

"I think my message is, 'Stick to your course,'" Vanderkaay said. "A lot of the reasons I've had success is listening to my coach, staying the course and believing in myself. You have to be patient in a sport like swimming where you don't get results immediately."

So having Vanderkaay for the 800 free was a bonus for Phelps as he moved down events in China. Later that night, just after 8 p.m., Michael still had the preliminaries for the 200 IM to get through. Had he and Bowman chosen to keep the 200 back in his schedule, it would have occurred a mere hour later.

However, in his solitary event of the evening, Phelps went a cruise-control speed of 1:58.5 to advance to the semifinals.

Phelps shared with the media one of the ways he stays grounded, a text message from a friend, which he retrieved during a press conference after the race and read.

"He said, 'Dude, it's ridiculous how many times a day I have to see your ugly face—keep up the good work,'" Phelps said. "And then his last one was, 'It's time to be the best ever.' That was the last text I saw this morning. Two of my friends got over here yesterday, and I was talking with them. They were saying people in the U.S. are just going crazy. One of my friends lives in New York, he said [Phelps is on] the cover of *The New York Times*. It's cool to have your country sort of by you and on your side. No matter where any Americans are in the world, they're watching, they're cheering, and it's a pretty special feeling."

Plus, Phelps had to hope Hansen was nearing top form, because that breaststroke leg on Phelps' eighth and final event, the 4×100 medley relay, was closing fast. Brendan Hansen is definitely the most alpha male of the Texas trio. While Peirsol can be found on the golf course and Crocker out working restoring an old car, cooking, or playing his guitar, Brendan is either out hunting for dinner or catching it. Hansen is never short on confidence.

Hansen, especially after he completed his degree at the University of Texas, spent a lot of time fishing, often with teammate Neil Walker, a multiple Olympian and multi-medal winner. The time with Walker probably serves to help Hansen to unwind. Garrett Weber-Gale, a 2008 Olympic teammate who also swims for University of Texas and trains with Hansen, has seen his teammate's intensity firsthand.

"Brendan can be really intense in practice," Weber-Gale said. "When he gets riled up about something, he's going to go flat-out until he drops."

Hansen is a thinker, and very practical—after turning professional, he bought his parents a gas fireplace for Christmas.

Hansen is from the small city of Havertown, Pennsylvania, with only 39,000 residents, seven miles from Philadelphia. His hometown is a Superfund site, which came about because of the town's timber mill that was used to finish telephone polls. The chemical used to coat the poles leaked into the ground.

Hansen is used to making due with the circumstances he faces, even if it leaves a sour taste in his mouth, sometimes literally: Once while growing up, his mother forgot to put sugar in a Thanksgiving Day pumpkin pie. He said he had seen how hard his mother worked that day making a great meal and desserts, so he just choked it down.

"The next year when Mom was making pumpkin

pie, we were like, 'Hey, Mom, does that have sugar?' " Hansen recalls.

While his mother blew the pie that one Thanksgiving Day, she and his father made all the right decisions in how to raise their children.

"It's been a part of all of my successes—a key to success," Hansen said of his upbringing. "I can only put in so much, so at some point I will break down, will need that boost, encouragement and support. To have your family there to back you up and offer some guidance: 'Why is it you are doing this? What's the goal? What's the big picture?' The thing is, my family has never forced me to swim, they've always made it my choice, and then they've supported me and encouraged me. My family saw that in swimming, I think early on, that I could learn from it about life. That if you want things in life, just like in the water, you have to work hard for it—it'll never be handed for you. You have to go after it."

One hobby he has that he does not want publicity about is visiting sick children in the hospital. He does it regularly in Austin.

"I won't make this a public event," Hansen said. "I've built a little platform where maybe I can help these kids—affect them in a positive way. You can't look into these kids' eyes without wanting to do something for them. They are very special and this means a lot to me."

He said Peirsol and Crocker, who have also done

the hospital visits with him, think it's important to be good role models.

"I just think there aren't enough good role models in the world today, especially in the world of sports," Hansen said. "Ian, Aaron and I talk about this—we want to be there for the kids because there is a lack of role models. It doesn't take a lot of effort to do the right thing. A lot of it has to do with how you are brought up—your values, character—that's part of my message to kids, that your closest role models are, or should be, your parents or brother or sister or someone else close to you."

While Hansen has set world records and won gold medals at the World Championships, Olympic gold has eluded him in the individual events. Japanese breaststroker, Kosuke Kitajima, won both breaststroke gold medals, and would eventually own both world records.

Still, Hansen used the silver in the 100 breaststroke and the 200 breaststroke bronze medal from Athens to motivate him, and pointed out that he still had a lot of good memories from the 2004 Games.

"It was great," Hansen said of the experience. "It's one of those things I will never forget. To do it with six guys from my team at Texas, and with the class of those guys—that's what I will never forget—to swim with the guys that I did is what means so much, not just the medals we brought home, but that we really were so close as a team."

The gold-medal-winning relay from that year included Hansen, Crocker and Peirsol, and knowing each other so well certainly played into their relay success.

"It was one of those things where everyone asks me or thinks that when you get that caliber of athletes together that others might not help out," Hansen said. "But the truth was we were helping each other—everyone on that team—from the first training camp in Stanford and onto Spain and into Athens. We were helping each other every day—everyone had something they did well, that they could offer suggestions or help someone else on. In fact, that's probably what won the 800 relay for us, having worked with each other to make us the best possible—and that's why we medaled in every event, except the one freestyle."

Hansen said achieving a certain level of fame is nice, but he knows how to keep focused. He even has fan Web sites that are maintained by his faithful following.

"Coming off the Olympics, people recognize me now—recognition I never had to this degree before," Hansen said. "But if you saw the group I hang out with, which includes Ian and Aaron—and my family—it's not hard for me to stay grounded. Actually, it's easy. So I won't change much."

Hansen said the key to a successful relay is realizing it is about more than just one person.

"Someone who can feed off the other three people,

who can realize that working as a team is more important than trying to do it all yourself," Hansen said. "When Ian, Aaron, me and Jason [Lezak] do a relay, we look at it as a team effort, 'How will we do?' not 'How fast is my own split going to be?'"

While the Japanese swimmer dominated the event and claimed his world record, Hansen learned firsthand at the 2008 Olympic Trials that anyone can win at any time. He made the team in just the 100 breaststroke, finishing fourth at Trials in the 200. But he is never one to look over his shoulder.

"That always comes up—that's what keeps you motivated," Hansen said. "That's always a possibility and you think about that a lot when you are training and it helps you get better. I'm hoping to get better."

Chapter 16

Thursday, August 14: No Finals, but Little Time to Rest

With an extra hour of rest, Phelps hit the water at 11:16 a.m. for the semifinals of the 200 IM, one of his signature events. He earned the top seed at 1:57.70, the only swimmer to break 1:58, and just ahead of Hungary's Laszlo Cseh, who in any other Olympics would have had his own collection of gold medals and the world's attention.

Phelps' day was not over. Later that evening, at 8:19, the prelims for the 100 butterfly—what would be the final event of Phelps individually for the Olympics—got underway.

"I think this being my third Olympics, I've been able to be in these situations a number of times—not only Olympics, but world championships," Phelps said. "I've been in big meets before. I sort of know how to, I guess, conserve my energy throughout a whole meet, whether it's seven days or nine days. That's probably the biggest thing that I've learned over the last four years is really just to be able to conserve my energy. It's pretty big when you get to this level, you have so many events, it's one of the most important things."

But in the heats that night, Serbian standout Milorad Cavic set an Olympic record and beat Phelps in their heat, with Cavic going 50.76 and Phelps 50.87. Medals are not won in prelims, but it was a message that a lot of people heard. Leading into the Olympics, Cavic, who lived in Anaheim, Calif., and trained in the Race Club, had been called "the guy who is going to upset Michael Phelps in the 100-meter butterfly" by his teammate, Gary Hall, Jr.

Also to consider was Phelps' teammate Ian Crocker, the world record-holder in the event, and someone Phelps would have to count on in the preliminaries of the final relay, the 4×100 medley relay.

Without Ian Crocker, Brendan Hansen and Aaron Peirsol, neither 2004 nor 2008 would have resulted in gold for Phelps.

Ian Crocker is the quiet, thoughtful one of the trio. Ian roomed with Brendan Hansen while they were freshmen at Texas. Ian would strum his guitar, and have college girls in the dorm come flocking to the room, swooning over his playing talent and reflective personality. One of his favorite guitars is one that former Olympic teammate, Gary Hall, Jr., gave Ian after the 2000 Olympics in Sydney.

Crocker does other events (he qualified to swim the 100 freestyle in the Athens Olympics individually for the United States), but he specializes in the 100 butterfly. And he does it well. He still has the world record, even though Phelps beat him at the Olympics in 2004. After that race, Phelps, who as the second-seeded American had swum the prelim relay but was then entitled to swim the finals after winning the individual event while Crocker took silver, gave his spot in the final to Crocker, who combined with Peirsol, Hansen and Lezak for gold. Phelps got gold for his prelim swim. Crocker also swam the prelims for the 4×100 medley relay in Beijing.

While his friends talk about hopping on a jet and seeing the world or getting a boat and traversing the ocean, Crocker never had such goals.

"Well, before Ian Crocker has time to go on a vacation like that, first he buys a '66 Cadillac convertible. And then he drives all over the country. That's what he would like to do," Crocker said, referring to himself in the third person. That makes sense—if you ever see Ian Crocker with a couple of magazines under his arm, they are likely *Hot Rod* magazine and *Car Craft*, and when he's retired, he hopes to be restoring old cars.

If Crocker were not a swimmer, he would like to be a drag racer, and while many think of scoreboard lights, Crocker is into the "Christmas tree" that starts an NHRA race. Crocker doesn't see himself as the macho, action-hero type alter-ago that a lot of athletes fashion themselves as. Rather, Crocker said he'd be cast as "the cowardly lion in *The Wizard of Oz*. I love his character." A devout Christian, Crocker enjoyed history and English while completing his degree at the University of Texas at Austin. He is known as being the best barbecue cook in the Longhorn program, and anyone who gets invited to Crocker's house for an outdoor dinner is in for quite a feast.

"Most people don't know that Ian is an outstanding cook, especially on the grill and the smoker," said Texas swimmer and Olympic teammate Garrett Weber-Gale. "I have been to his house numerous times for dinner. One time he smoked two big chickens and he stuffed some sort of spiced cream cheese between the skin and meat. It was so good I ended up eating most of both chickens."

Crocker is also into photography and takes his camera everywhere, with his favorite subjects either the great outdoors or car shows.

He was so slow starting out as a swimmer growing up in his home state of Maine that he had to go to a special group that taught how to do the strokes as an 8-year-old before he was accepted into practice with the team at the local YMCA. "I was that bad," he said with a smile.

Not for long. After 2004, Ian Crocker had Olympic medals of all colors, and the world record in the 100 butterfly.

Chapter 17

Friday, August 15: Finals, 200 Individual Medley

Michael Phelps had a busy Friday. While the talk was about Cavic, most of it was coming from Cavic. He had given up the 100 freestyle to focus all of his energy on taking down Phelps in the 100 butterfly and winning gold.

Phelps, however, was not giving up his other events, and he started out Friday with another world record, 1:54.23, good for the gold medal in the 200 IM and more than two seconds better than silver medal-winning Laszlo Cseh. Phelps' teammate Ryan Lochte was third for the bronze medal.

"I just wanted to step on it in the first 50 a little bit and get out to an early lead," said Phelps, whose wins that week also include the 400m IM, the 400m free relay, the 200m free, the 200m fly and the 200m IM. "I knew in the first half that if I got a big enough lead I could hang on, and that's all I wanted to do."

Though he set another record, Phelps admits he was keeping in mind not to run his fuel tank dry.

"The next two races are pretty important," Phelps said. "I have to conserve as much physical and emotional energy as I can."

Later that night in China, Milorad Cavic sent another not-so-subtle message.

"It would be good for the sport if he loses," Cavic said. "It'd be good for him if he loses. It would be nice if historians talk about Michael Phelps winning seven gold medals and losing the eighth to 'some guy.' I'd like to be that guy."

Since he and Phelps had been the top two in the prelims, each would be the top seed in separate semifinals. Cavic posted the fastest time and took the top seed. Phelps went 50.97 seconds to win the first semifinal, while Cavic went 50.92 to claim the second semifinal and was ranked first for the final.

Phelps was also counting on Peirsol, who lost on the same day to Lochte in the 200 backstroke, though Peirsol did get a silver medal to add to the gold he had won earlier in the week in the 100 backstroke.

Aaron Peirsol is the "surfer dude" out of the Texas trio of himself, Crocker and Hansen. Peirsol is praised throughout the swimming community for being a good teammate, always being laid-back outside of the pool, and always being ready to race in the water.

He also volunteers to speak about environmental causes related to the oceans. Being a spokesman for open water is something he takes seriously.

"You don't want to look back years from now and say, 'What did we do [to our environment]? This is something we could've gotten around. We could've found another way,'" Aaron says. "Yes, sometimes, people are a little single-minded in what they do and what they want, as far as the environment goes. They don't give a well-thought-out plan to what effect it will have long-term."

Peirsol is a reliable relay teammate. He said he gets up in the morning when he's tired, he goes in "knowing the other guys will be there too, going through the same thing I'm facing. You build up this certain camaraderie and support for the people you swim with," Peirsol said. "You build that confidence that you belong there, that you belong with the best. We realized that many years ago when we were a lot younger, so it became a matter of, 'How far can we push it?' We get together on a relay, and it's not, 'Can we win?' but 'How much can we win by?' That's our mentality for the relay. We're all very different personalities too, which makes it kind of cool. We all have something different to bring to the table, and we're all very effective individually. So that also makes it pretty unique."

Probably the most remarkable thing about the Peirsol family is that, as laid-back as Aaron is, his sister Hayley—a standout swimmer who has made international teams and was part of the national championship run at Auburn—is just the opposite: really wound up. In fact, as a child, Hayley was always messing with Aaron, often just for the sake of messing with him.

"When we were young, really little—Hayley called the cops when she and I were having a disagreement," Aaron says. "She was five, and I was seven. She was crazy. I still remember it to this day. The police actually showed up at our house over this disagreement between brother and sister."

Hayley admitted it happened just as her brother said.

"I was such a little hellion," Hayley says. "I could literally do anything and get away with it. I would run to my grandpa and tell him that Aaron was hitting me just to see Grandpa give Aaron the talk. Aaron really did have to put up with quite a bit. And I do remember calling the police. He told you the story correctly. We were just sitting at home, and somehow he made me mad. I told him that I could call the cops on him and they'd come get him. He told me he didn't believe I'd call the police. 'Oh yes, I will,' I told him. And I did. I came back and sat down, and Aaron said, 'Oh my gosh, you actually did it!' But I really only did it to prove him wrong—that I would do it. But we were both in shock that I did it. You can imagine my parents' reaction when they got home. Poor Aaron—he did put up with a lot!"

The two are close, and when Hayley helped spark Auburn's national title win over defending champion Georgia, Aaron was there.

"Man, it was surreal," Aaron says. "I knew Hayley was swimming well all year. A couple of years ago she had gone through a little funk, so I wanted to see her at NCAAs. I needed to be there. I wanted to be there, I mean. I was so glad to see her swim like that. Watching her race, I was just so proud of her. To win the way she did, it was like you will yourself past someone in a sense, and that's the kind of win that is most rewarding. She definitely earned that win. I'm just so proud of her."

In fact, Aaron even bought his sister a Marc Jacobs designer bag, something she said was among her favorite presents ever.

Having the means to buy his sister nice things has been one of the perks of being a professional swimmer. He said the money is nice, but it has not affected who he is—just how he spends, and what he buys.

"Maybe it's changed me, but not for the worse," Aaron says. "You have different responsibilities, but nothing too drastic. I've never swum for the glory. You do this, and it's pretty cool to make a living and have an impact doing the sport you grew up in."

During an interview, Peirsol was asked what animal he'd rather be chased by, a bear or a tiger—it was a question in the USA Swimming 20 Question Tuesday that was a staple, just a sort of "for fun" question. Peirsol had the best answer.

"Can I pick neither?" Peirsol says. "I guess a tiger, because it's cool looking. But either way, face it—you're done."

Having Crocker and Hansen—also world-record holders in the butterfly and breaststroke at the time, respectively—as teammates at the University of Texas helped all three stayed focused.

"It's a common bond, an understanding that everyone else understands what the motivation and goals are," Aaron said. "Having everyone at the same level really helps all of us."

Peirsol bought some property in the Central American country of Costa Rica. Though he says Australia is his favorite place to visit because "there's just nothing wrong with Australia," he'll more likely be seen on his surfboard catching coastal Costa Rican waves after he retires, because he never was sure exactly where he wanted to live post-retirement from swimming, just "somewhere close to the beach."

Peirsol said his Costa Rica place is something out of dreams.

"It's beautiful," he says. "We have a place about an hour south of a town. Where we're at, there are no paved roads and very little running water. We're building on our land there now, and it's looking pretty cool."

He also knows a lot about science. His favorite subject in college was biology, though he loves physics, too.

"I just love to know how things work and why," he says.

After dominating his events at the 2004 Olympics, he returned to the pool and bettered his own record times at non-Olympic meets. He said it wasn't his goal to set records only at the Olympics.

"I don't know. I've never really seen an Olympic year as being an end-of-a-season thing, or an end-of-four-years or end of anything," Peirsol said. "You try to get better. I don't put much stock into taking a break and coming back in two years in time for the Olympics. When I want to be done with the sport, I'll be done with it. There's no point in waiting around for that special moment to occur once every four years. The way I look at it is that if tomorrow I swam that one race I felt I could never swim again, I could hand in my suit. I don't have to do that race at the Olympics. I just want that one swim I can look back on and be proud of, and then, that'll be enough for me."

Aaron was disqualified after winning the 200 backstroke in Athens right after the race. While officials conferred, he just smiled and said he had no regrets, that he thought he hadn't done anything wrong and that he could live with whatever officials decided because he knew the truth. The officials huddled and overruled the one of them who thought Peirsol had used an improper technique, and he was awarded the gold medal he had earned. He said he gets that attitude from how he was raised.

"I definitely get that from my parents," Peirsol says. "Everyone is a product of the people they are raised by, or grow up with. That said, once your values are instilled, the rest is up to you. Specifically to the question about that moment at the Olympics: under the circumstances, I knew I had won and done nothing wrong. As long as the guys in the race felt the same way—that I did nothing wrong—then if I don't get the medal, yeah, it's a bummer, but I knew I'd be just fine. So I just headed to the warm-up pool because I knew I had done nothing wrong. It wasn't the medal I was going after, it was the swim that I had, and I was very proud of that. Of course," he laughs, "it was nice they reviewed it and I received the gold."

Before the Olympics, Peirsol was sent to China on a goodwill sort of trip to generate interest in the upcoming Games and to help introduce the West to today's China.

"Dude, China was awesome," Aaron says. "It was one of my best trips in a long time. It was a very different, eye-opening experience. I know I'll be going back. I recommended it to all the guys. Yeah, are you kidding me? For sure. It wasn't just seeing the venues for 2008, it was about the culture, and that was so cool. Beijing is actually a pretty Westernized city, but the rest of China isn't as much. The rest of the country, the parts I was fortunate enough to visit, were just great. China will field some of the best swimmers in 2008 at their Olympics. They will put on a show, I'm saying that right now."

One of Peirsol's biggest fans is also one of his top U.S. competitors: his 2008 Olympic teammate, Matt Grevers.

"Aaron Peirsol. I don't understand the guy because he's so fast and talented, but he's really a relaxed person," Grevers says with a laugh. "That's just not usually what you see in a competitor. Behind the blocks, guys try to act friendly, but Aaron Peirsol really is, and means it. He's rooting for you. He's my favorite swimmer."

Teammate Garrett Weber-Gale has spent a lot of time with Peirsol at the University of Texas, and agrees Peirsol's "coolness" is no act.

"Aaron is the most laid-back person I have ever known," Weber-Gale says. "I don't think there is much that really stresses him out or frazzles him. He is, for sure, a California surfer dude."

While a lot of young up-and-coming swimmers threatened to knock him off for one of the two spots in the 100 and 200 backstrokes—Phelps was scheduled to try for a backstroke spot before the

2004 Olympics before reconsidering—Peirsol does not give a lot of thought to his competition.

"I've never been the kind to do that," Peirsol says. "The guys I compete against now, like Michael Phelps or Ryan Lochte, these aren't even their main events. But I've never been the kind to do that, even when a meet is coming up, or whatever. You go out, do your best race, and that's it."

Plus, having the world records and gold medals is something he really takes pride in. Though he did check his medals with his baggage at the airport on the way home from an international competition, and his bag was temporarily lost, he got the bag and the medals back eventually.

"It's cool—I mean, to set a record, to win gold and be the best—that's something no one can ever take away from you," Peirsol says.

A feeling Phelps could no doubt relate to—but not before he took care of some more business.

Chapter 18

Saturday, August 16: Finals, 100 Butterfly

The schedule lightened up on Saturday for Phelps and all swimmers in terms of volume. But for Michael Phelps and the millions following him, the intensity would never be higher.

Bowman relayed the predictions that Cavic would win the gold.

"When people say things like that, it fires me up more than anything," Phelps says. "Just like 400 free relay going into that, we were excited because the French swimmers had said a few remarks that got us a little excited. We use things like that and comments like that to fuel us. To get us more excited. I think that's what American swimmers do. We rise to the occasion. When Bob told me that, actually this morning, I said, 'Okay, we'll let our swimming do the talking.' That's how I've always done it. I always welcome comments. If anyone wants to say anything, I like it. It definitely motivates me even more."

Phelps knew going into the final he could not do what he had done in Athens, where he came back to edge Crocker after Phelps was only in fifth place at the turn. That would not do tonight, not with Cavic—and Crocker—in the finals.

So what did Phelps do? He got off to an even slower start. He was seventh—out of eight—at the turn, and it looked like all hope was lost. He closed the distance down as they went home the last 10 meters, with Cavic clearly ahead. But with three meters to go, Phelps clicked into a higher gear, and made the odd move of throwing his arms out for a "chop" or "half" stroke to propel him to the wall. By the time his hands were coming forward, Cavic was already gliding, arm outstretched, just inches from the wall. But the momentum and arm speed Phelps had generated with that last partial stroke threw his hand into the wall, like a truck slamming into it.

Everyone looked at the clock. While it appeared to the casual eye that Cavic had easily won, the scoreboard gave the times. Phelps had won, by one one-hundredth of a second. That last push, that last burst, had given him the win.

"When I took that last half-stroke, I thought I lost the race right there, but it turns out that was the difference," Phelps says. "I'm just at a loss for words. I feel a little bit of everything—relief, excitement, everything. I had to take my goggles off to make sure the number 1 was next to my name. When I saw that '1' next to my name, that's when I sort of let my roar out."

A protest was filed by the Serbian team. Cavic's coach for the meet was Race Club coach Mike Bottom, who in another irony was to succeed Bob Bowman as head coach at the University of Michigan and Club Wolverine, Phelps' team the past four years.

"It was very clear that [Cavic] touched second behind Michael Phelps," FINA referee Ben Ekumbo said. "One was stroking while the other was gliding."

Cavic was proud of his effort.

"Losing by one one-hundredth of a second is the most difficult loss, especially at the Olympics," Cavic said. "And I did see the replays, but if you are asking that I'm disappointed? It's a complete miracle to me that I am here, and I retired a year and a half ago and I came back to swimming thinking I wasn't good enough to compete at this level and at this competition. I'm enjoying this. From my heart, I am really enjoying this moment. I wish I were a gold medalist, but you know I'll take a silver medal. I'm very comfortable with this."

The protest was filed. FINA, the sport's governing body, looked at video from the cameras placed on poles right above the end, which provide a backup for the touchpads, which listed Phelps as the winner by .01 of a second. The cameras backed it up—Phelps had won. For the second consecutive Olympics, Phelps had won the 100 meter butterfly by one one-hundredth of a second.

Cavic said he hoped people would forget about the protest that had been filed and denied, and focus on the race.

"I'm stoked with what happened," Cavic said. "I'm very, very happy. I don't want to fight this. It is a difficult thing to lose, but you have to understand that I came into this competition with a goal to win a bronze medal. I went my best time, and I did better than bronze—I got silver, and I almost got gold. For me to end my career right now, if this is what I decide to do, I will be completely happy."

The race—except the ending—unfolded exactly how Cavic had planned.

"I knew I was leading the race, I usually do, and I've been training all year," Cavic said. "I know I'm fast the first fifty. I knew I was going to lead the first fifty and I know that Michael's a back half swimmer and that he was going to be chasing me down in the end. So, the last fifteen meters, there was just no point to look over. I knew he was there. Just from my recollection, I don't actually remember looking, I just saw a shadow out of the side of my goggles, and I knew he was coming. It's a good thing for myself because I like to be chased. When I know someone is chasing me I always seem to give a little bit extra. The last fifteen meters, especially the last eight, I just put my head down and I did not breathe the last eight meters. I was just hoping for the best."

It was close, but the Omega cameras showed that by the distance of less than a fingernail, Phelps had made it to the wall first.

"The timing system says it all," Phelps says. "There hasn't really been an error in the timing system that I remember. I have no idea. The only thing I can say is I raced as hard as I could and I swam my best. The scoreboard said I got my hand on the wall first."

Cavic said while technology is imperfect, slowing it down so much gave a clearer picture.

"You know, the hand is quicker than the eye, I suppose," Cavic said. "But . . . I overheard Michael Phelps talk about how Mark Schubert went into the video room and they were filming it to the thousandth of a second, and he said it was crazy. It was just a crazy finish. It's too bad that we both couldn't have finished at 50.58. I would have loved to share that gold medal, but I'm taking what I got and I'm happy."

While Internet-conspiracy theorists jumped off their couches and into action faster than dot-com start-ups, Cavic was gracious. He accepted the decision, as did his coaches, and FINA had the evidence from the touchpad, the timer and the Omega cameras.

At the post-race press conference, a member of the media asked Cavic how he felt beating Phelps. Cavic corrected the reporter.

"He probably didn't say it very well, but I didn't beat Phelps," Cavic replied. "Perhaps I was the only guy at this competition who had a real shot at beating Phelps one-on-one. This is completely new to me, I've never been in such a position with so much pressure, and I am very proud of how I handled that whole race and how I was able to keep myself under control emotionally and the stress level. It is a frightening thing to know that you're racing Michael Phelps, but I think that it's even more frightening to know that it's going to be a very, very close race and that nobody knows the outcome. I read a lot of articles online. I like to read them—it encourages me and I knew a lot of people had their money against me. That was totally understandable. Michael has been breaking world records here by seconds. This is something that no other swimmer in swimming really does, so what do you expect from a man who breaks world records by seconds in the 100 fly? You know, I expected that he'd go a world record time— maybe something close, like 50.2. But it was a real honor for me to be able to race with Michael Phelps and be in this situation where all eyes were on me as the one man that would possibly be able to do it. It was just great."

It was unthinkable to those who watched in real-time that Cavic did not win. But slowed down frame by frame, FINA officials confidently told the world that there was no doubt all the equipment was right, that Michael Phelps was seven-for-seven in events and gold medals.

"I saw the race actually afterward," Phelps said. "I saw the finish on the big screen after race. I saw it slowed down frame-by-frame back in the massage area, looking at the computer. It's almost too close to see. It's sort of like last time [in Athens] I felt four one-hundredths was close; I was completely shocked. It's possible I'm even more shocked now than I was then. One one-hundredth is the smallest margin in our sport. It was pretty cool. I guess that's all I can say."

Michael Phelps had done it. Seven gold medals in seven events. He had joined the company of Mark Spitz, who had admitted it was kind of lonely at the top and he wouldn't mind some company as long as it was of the caliber of someone like Michael Phelps.

But Phelps was hoping for a one-day membership only.

He had another club to join—one he could create himself.

Because the next day brought a chance for one more gold medal—his eighth.

And a chance to be in a league all his own. He'd need some help from his relay buddies, though.

The U.S. swim teams take great pride in their

relays. For this Olympics, it was the U.S. men who were at the top of their game.

The one event remaining at the Water Cube for Michael Phelps was not an easy one. The relay is the least forgiving of errors, as the U.S. had realized a year earlier when the team was disqualified at the 2007 World Championships in Melbourne, Australia.

The 400 medley relay is 100 meters of each stroke—backstroke, breaststroke, butterfly and freestyle—from each swimmer. As the current swimmer comes to the wall and touches, the next swimmer's toes still have to be on the block. The exchange time can be as low as .00—and there is a touch-pad timing system set up on the block to measure the difference. The key was not to have that exchange be in the negative like it was in 2007.

"I'm happy, but it's not over yet," Phelps said. "I think the Australian team looks really great for tomorrow. It's going to be a race. I'm looking forward to it."

There was a lot of reason for concern for the Americans. First and foremost, there was the team in the lane next to them—Australia. Since Ian Thorpe had retired and Grant Hackett had been nursing injuries, Australia had found itself on the outside looking in as countries like France and Japan had joined the Americans in getting a lot of media attention in men's swimming at these Games. Knocking off the Americans and preventing Michael Phelps from winning his eighth gold medal would help the Australians salvage their reputation as the world's swimming powerhouse and take something to rebuild from at the 2008 Olympic Games in Beijing.

"Tomorrow is definitely not going to be an easy race," Phelps said. "Australia has a very good relay. We're going to do like we did the last two relays. It's all about being a team. We're going to go out there as a team and swim as a team. We'll be able to swim as a team. That's not a problem. Hopefully we're able to put four amazing splits together and see what happens."

Chapter 19

Sunday, August 17: Finals, 4 × 100 Medley Relay

With all due respect to Australia, the Americans had their own problems. Phelps was coming off an emotional win in the 100 butterfly the night before, and while he had won gold, for the first time in these Games he had not set a world record, or even an American or Olympic record, with his time. A half-second in a relay like this could be enough to push them to second place.

And Phelps was actually the least of their worries. Brendan Hansen, who had dominated the 100 and 200 breaststrokes in previous world competitions, and medaled at the 2004 Olympics, did not even qualify for the 200 breaststroke in China. And in the 2008 Olympic 100 breaststroke, Hansen did not medal, and did not even look like a shade of his former self, taking a quiet fourth place.

Aaron Peirsol, after winning the 100 backstroke, though unable to defend his Olympic gold in the 200 backstroke after that, had hit his elbow at the wall, and was nursing that.

And Jason Lezak had given all he had time and again for the United States, with that best-ever effort—for himself and the world—in the final leg of the 4×100 freestyle relay, keeping Phelps' bid for eight golds alive earlier in the week. But how much could Lezak, at age 32, possibly have left?

Worse than that, he had a hungry Australian he'd have to face, Eamon Sullivan, one of the favorites to win the 100 freestyle who had taken silver instead, and was ready to redeem himself going head-to-head with Lezak on the anchor leg if it came down to that.

The starting buzzer sounded, and in less than four minutes all of the questions would be answered. The world would know whether Michael Phelps would solidify himself as the greatest of all time by getting his eighth gold medal, separating him from even the legendary seven golds of Mark Spitz.

The Water Cube was as loud as ever, as Peirsol did his job with a solid 100 backstroke, his split of 53.16 seconds giving the U.S. a half-second lead over Australia and Japan.

Hansen was up next. The Texas teammate of Peirsol—and Ian Crocker—went 59.28, and Australia had made up the deficit and more with Brenton Rickard's breaststroke time of 58.56 seconds. Japan had hammered 1.2 seconds off the U.S. on the breaststroke.

The American bid was in trouble.

Phelps was next, and he'd have to find a time around 51 seconds to keep the Americans in it. Phelps got nearly a full second back with his 50.15 seconds, and it would be up to Lezak to, in effect, hold off Australia with the eight-tenths-of-a-second. Japan was closer at that point, but its final sprinter wasn't at the level of either Sullivan or Lezak.

For the second time in these Games, Lezak went under 47 seconds in a 100 relay, going 46.76 seconds, holding off a charging Sullivan, who went 46.65, just over a tenth better than Lezak—but it wasn't enough.

Lezak hit the wall to give the Americans the world record—and gold medal—at 3:29.34, with Sullivan's outstanding effort good for a time of 3:30.04, and the silver medal. Japan was third.

Once again, Jason Lezak had saved the day.

"I was just trying not to blow the lead, to be honest," Lezak said. "I was really nervous. I didn't go in [to the 400m free relay] expecting to beat Bernard, and I knew Eamon was capable of doing the same thing to me. I just wanted to take it out hard and hoped to hold on."

Michael Phelps had eight gold medals.

"I can't say it enough," Phelps said. "I've been fairly speechless since the relay. It's all been a dream come true. To be able to imagine something and work towards it and accomplish everything you ever dreamed of, it's fun. These guys made it possible. The relay really made it possible. It shows how much teamwork and togetherness we have. It's amazing to be a part of it. I wanted to do something that no one's ever done in this sport, and without the help of my teammates, it wouldn't have been possible. I have all the memories and the pictures. I'll have all the medals, every suit, every cap, my award sweats, but the best memories for meets like this are spent with your teammates, playing Spades with them, playing [the board game] Risk and just getting to know them. To be a part of Team USA is one of the best memories I'll take away from this."

Thorpe said he was proud of Phelps, and that his comments leading up to the Olympics—about how he did not think Phelps could win seven or eight gold medals—was misinterpreted.

"I said that I didn't think he would, I never said he wouldn't," Thorpe told the London *Telegraph*. "I just couldn't envision it happening. And I didn't think he would get all eight, not because Michael couldn't win, but because of the competition. It's been a very tough week to get through. I couldn't do it. You couldn't imagine much closer races. The 4×100 free goes down as one of the all-time great races. And coming down the last length of the 100 fly as well. Never in my life have I been so happy to have been proved wrong. I enjoyed every moment of it."

In a live split-screen interview on NBC, Spitz, who was back in the United States, was very gracious to Phelps, who was also respectful of Spitz.

"I wondered what I was going to say at this monumental time," Spitz told Phelps. "The word that comes to mind: *Epic*. What you did was epic."

Chapter 20

U.S. Women Make Their Own History

While Michael Phelps' performance was one for the ages, several members of the U.S. Olympic women's swimming team also turned in noteworthy performances—one ageless, and another for the ages. Natalie Coughlin, Rebecca Soni and Dara Torres all turned in incredible Olympic performances, though outside of the expansive cover of Torres, Coughlin and Soni received comparatively little news coverage, despite providing a couple of the best all-around stories at the Games.

Perhaps the quietest—but now the most decorated—American women's swimmer is Natalie Coughlin. She won six Olympic medals in Beijing, and to even make the team in several events, had to go against the best in the world.

Coughlin's medals included gold in the 100

backstroke, silver in the 400 medley relay (which included Soni and Torres), silver in the 400 freestyle relay (which included Torres), bronze in the 100 free, bronze in the 800 freestyle relay, and bronze in the 200 IM, where she beat American Katie Hoff, who had won the event at Trials.

A graduate of Cal-Berkeley, Coughlin has interests outside of the pool that mean as much to her as her life in the water. She goes out of her way to keep balance in her life, and while swimmers everywhere do doubles and train hours every single day, Coughlin is just as prone to balance a single daily workout with Pilates, walking her dog She-Ra, or spinning.

Coughlin learned training from Cal coach Teri McKeever, an Olympic assistant coach. She discovered that more is not always better in terms of training in the pool, so her routine changed to focus more on dryland training.

"It's much, much different—a lot more training out of the pool than I was used to," Coughlin says. "I never really did weights, or at least not the weights I'm doing now. The in-pool stuff was more distance-oriented and volume back then, which was great for me at that time. But now it's much more race-specific, a lot of race quality in practice."

Coughlin especially enjoys time in the kitchen, wine collecting, and at times has been passionate about photography.

"There are so many hobbies I'd love to do. A lot

of people know I'm really into cooking and photography—photography having been kind of rejuvenated the last couple of years," Coughlin says. "I was very into it, but couldn't afford a good digital camera when those first came out, and I can now. So I have a good camera. Also, I would love to learn a couple of languages, but most of those classes are five days a week, and with my schedule I can't do that right now—not if I want to make the commitment to it that it deserves."

Just like Michael Phelps is a big fan of the Baltimore Ravens, Coughlin has similar passion for her team, the Oakland Raiders.

Though she has that balance, she knows her dedication to sports has provided her with a good lifestyle, one that allows her the time and means to pursue other interests.

She can be seen winning medals in the pool one day and shopping at a store with a former Cal teammate the following week. But don't think the fact that she likes to shop means she spends marathon time at the mall.

"I'm a very quick shopper," Coughlin says. "I'm one of those people who, when I like what I see, I buy it immediately. So I can be in and out in two hours and have tons of stuff."

She also has some interior-design skills. She decorated the place she bought near school after turning professional as a swimmer.

"I enjoyed buying everything," Coughlin says. "I did these built-in cabinets in my dining room. They are mahogany, and beautiful. I have a Sub-Zero refrigerator, and my dining room is very elegant. On my terrace, I have a few citrus trees and an herb garden, so I love eating out there. I even got a patio heater so I can turn that on in the winter and still spend a lot of time out there."

Coughlin says she appreciates seeing young swimmers who are inspired by Olympians. But true to her own philosophy, she says they should have fun first, and realize that what they learn in the water can also make their lives on solid ground better, too.

"Set goals and challenge yourself, but realize that it's a fine line to balance to where you take it too seriously," Natalie says. "Don't let it consume you, and enjoy it and learn as you go. The key point is, first of all, to love what you do and do what you love. Second of all, it's to realize that with success you have to experience failure. Success is that much more meaningful when you have the experience of failure, or just the ups and downs—the big challenges. When you experience failure, it can and should make you better."

Coughlin might stick around a while longer. She's still having fun.

"As long as I'm injury-free and enjoying the

sport," Coughlin says, "I see myself continuing to swim."

Dara Torres is a different breed, plain and simple. A model and celebrity racer, Torres has done it all. Though she got a lot of attention for the amazing accomplishment of her fifth Olympic Games, people often forget that in addition to skipping the 2004 Olympics because she was retired, she had also "retired" before the 1996 Atlanta Games, so she could have easily been in her seventh Olympics when she dove into the pool in Beijing. In all five of her Olympics, she has medaled.

Torres also brought to China prayers for her coach, Michael Lohberg, who was battling a life-threatening illness diagnosed in 2008 just before the Olympics.

The "gray-haired" member of the team—though Dara certainly does not have any gray hair in a literal sense—Torres had a mane full of silver medals after the Olympics, winning a pair of relay silver medals. She also won a silver medal in her only individual event, the 50 freestyle, where she set the American record but (in a reversal of what happened to Phelps) came in second in the 50 free by one hundredth of a second.

The elder stateswoman of U.S. swimming has

defied Father Time and been an inspiration to daughters and mothers around the world.

"It's funny because there are days when I don't feel forty at all—when I am swimming those races and going fast," Torres says. "But then there are days when I can't lift my arms up, and I realize I *am* forty!" Her daughter, Tessa, is probably too young to remember much about her mom's performance in China, but Dara says her daughter is definitely a reflection of herself.

"Tessa is awesome—she has so much energy," Dara says. "She's all over the place. God got even with me. She is definitely a Mini-Me."

Motherhood for her has been an eye-opener.

"I have to admit the first couple of weeks were really tough," Dara says. "I had no experience with kids, so you have to get used to the crying and what her needs are. After that, it's been sort of a breeze. You read baby books and everything, but you never know what it's like until they are born. It's awesome."

It was actually Tessa who got Dara back in the water—before Tessa was even born. "You know, I started swimming three months into being pregnant," Dara says. "It was something where I was trying to get [David] to swim again, so I said, 'Let's join a masters team.' I loved swimming again. After about six and a half to seven months, I had to stop traveling for my work, so I'd go at eight or nine in the morning—instead of five!—and my masters coach would leave me workouts. I had certain limits. The doctor said not to get too out of breath, because if you're out of breath, the baby can't breathe either. So we monitored everything. I ended up doing about three thousand meters three or four times a week. I really stuck with it. I went to swim one day, and then lifted and went that night in the hospital and delivered the next day. My first question after I saw [my baby] was healthy and I was holding her on my lap was, 'When can I swim again?' The doctor said I could lift again right away, but to wait four to six weeks to swim. Well, I had a swim meet coming up. A week and a half later, I saw a guy walk into the gym, and it was my doctor, and I said, 'Can I swim yet?' He said, 'You know what? Go ahead and swim if you feel like it. We really have no clue on how long you should wait. If you feel all right, and you're doing well, then go ahead.' So I started swimming again, and it felt so good."

Tessa was also Dara's inspiration—in addition to being her motivation—because after the 2000 Games in Australia, Dara was ready to retire, and this time stay retired.

"After Sydney, I always told myself that if I ever had a kid, I'd get back into swimming," Dara says. "Well, I had a kid, and I'm back swimming. But let me tell you, I had morning sickness and was nauseous for five and a half to six months, so there were some bad days in the pool."

While Dara had stayed in shape—and had gotten back into shape immediately after having Tessa, though many would argue she never got out of shape—Dara says her comeback was driven more by people her own age rather than the younger women she'd have to chase down to make the team.

"There are a lot of different elements," Dara says. "When I went to Masters World Championships, I had so many swimmers come up and say, 'It would be so nice to have someone our age swimming in the Olympics.' That motivated me. I was still breastfeeding and going those fast times, so I realized I could try it."

Tessa's father, and the rest of Dara's family, also provided some inspiration and encouragement.

"I have twenty nieces and nephews who are too young to have even seen me swim in 2000, so it's pretty special," Dara says. "My significant other, David, is like, 'I wish I would have known you when you swam.' So now he does."

Being older has helped her not lose focus or be overwhelmed by pressure, something she discovered at the 2007 Nationals.

"Here's a funny story: Before my first race at Nationals, I thought I was going to throw up," Dara said. "I think I ate the wrong thing. I had what I usually eat [a shake], but not with the lighter milk I usually drink, but a big glass of whole milk, and I felt so sick. If I had been eighteen and felt like that, I would have choked and not done well. I was able to stay calm and get through it. Age definitely plays a favor in a positive way, mentally."

Dara said it was at the Nationals where she finally believed that far more people were cheering for her than the vocal few who were claiming she could not have done this cleanly—even though she was a participant in a revolutionary drug-testing program that preserves samples to be tested as procedures improve in the future.

"It means so much to me," Dara says of the support. "I got up on blocks at Nationals, and they announced my name, and everyone was clapping. I was like, 'Who did they just announce? Are they clapping for me?' I did an appearance for Toyota there for the Engine of Change program, and it was a sixty-forty mix of adults and kids, whereas before it was one hundred percent kids. So it's really funny, and a nice little mix. But I did have some kids, too, who came up, so it's nice to see the younger kids might know who I am. I still can't explain it, the great feeling from the applause at Nationals. Unreal. All that clapping for me? Michael Phelps maybe, but not for me."

Like Coughlin, Dara subscribes to focusing on quality rather than quantity of training.

"The less you do, the faster you go—or that's what it is for me, right now, at my age and the shape I am, and the experience I have," Dara says. "I'm finally finding my rhythm of what to do, and what not to do."

Dara says that she is, like Coughlin, enjoying the wild ride that swimming has been for her.

"You know, I am just having a lot of fun," she says. "Swimming is a great sport for a lot of reasons—to stay in shape, and make friends. Going fast is fun, too."

While Natalie emerged as the most-decorated American female winner and Dara's career has a timelessness that is difficult to perceive, Rebecca Soni became the feel-good story of the Games.

Rebecca, coming off her junior year at the University of Southern California, was also coming off surgery to fix a heart problem. While she refers to it as a "minor" procedure, doctors everywhere said anything that involves the heart is a major concern.

The New Jersey native had a rapid-heartbeat condition at least monthly since turning 16 years old. She originally planned to have the surgery before going to USC, but decided against it since the condition was not worsening. But her first year at USC, the episodes started happening more often, with her heart peaking at 400 beats per minute. This would happen occasionally in practice her sophomore year, and was so severe she'd have to stop her workout. In 2006, she had surgery which destroyed tissue creating the problem around her heart.

"The last year has taught me a lot about how much swimming and competing mean to me," Rebecca told USA Swimming.

Rebecca won a gold medal and two silver medals in Beijing. She did not make the team in the 100 breaststroke, but was inserted into the opening created when a teammate failed a drug test. She delivered a silver in that event, the only American to medal in the 100 breaststroke in Beijing. Rebecca went one better than that in the 200 breaststroke. What was most impressive about that is she beat world-record holder Liesel Jones of Australia, and in the process, Soni set a world record.

"It definitely exceeded my expectations. I already have two medals and I only came for one event," Rebecca said after setting the record and claiming gold in the 200 breaststroke. "It feels great. It has been a long road to get here."

She followed that up on her final day of competition by teaming with Coughlin and Torres, and Christine Magnuson, to claim silver in the 400 medley relay.

For Rebecca, big meets aren't as big a deal as most people might think.

"Going into a meet, I just kind of try to keep my confidence high and tell myself that I can be as good as the people I'm racing with, and that I am one of the fastest," says Rebecca, whose sister Rita swam for Texas A&M. "But I definitely get really nervous before the race. Sitting in the ready room is the worst part, waiting to swim. I do enjoy it from the moment I get up on the blocks."

For the soft-spoken Rebecca, representing America means a lot, because neither her father nor mother were born in the U.S.

"Both of my parents are Hungarians, but they lived in Romania before coming here," she says. "I took growing up in that culture for granted, definitely, because I didn't realize what I had until I got older. The way we lived was definitely different. I'd notice that when I went to a friend's house. Our family was just so close. It's like a whole different environment, and I'm glad we were so close. I'm very fortunate with my family, and my parents. They've been very supportive of me, but never pushed me."

Chapter 21

Live, from China:
A Family Affair

Seeing Michael make history was quite an experience for his sisters and mother. But so was seeing China.

"A few things surprised me about China, but mainly the difference in culture," Hilary said. "Before we went, we read about the city and knew what to expect. But I don't think that anything could prepare us for the traffic and driving. We heard the statistic that there were only ten to fifty percent of the cars on the road, due to traffic control, but even at nine at night, the roads were packed and reminded me of being in a parking lot. They had a special Olympic lane, where only cars with Olympic permits could travel. We were fortunate to have traveled most of the time in those lanes. Getting a taxi was sometimes a challenge, and the drive was always a wild ride."

The trip did provide some scenic memories.

"Another amazement was seeing the Great Wall in person," Whitney said. "We took a trolley ride to the top and walked a couple of the gates. Standing up there and looking around it blew my mind that it was constructed by hand. As I looked around I saw people from all over the world and I had my husband, sister and cousins all experiencing this with me."

While Whitney, her sister and mother had fun in China, the food took a bit of getting used to, though through sponsor hospitality suites, they were able to get enough energy to cheer on Michael.

"It was different—it's always hard when you are overseas and used to American food, but we are always open to trying new things," Whitney said. "We went to the Omega House one day and had prawns—those were really good. We had a lot of meals in the VISA Hospitality area, which were awesome. When we had the chance to get American food we devoured it—it was great."

Whitney (Phelps) Flickinger said the attention from her "TV time" at the Olympics caught her off-guard.

"I was getting emails from coworkers and friends, 'You are on TV as much as Michael is'—so getting emails, I realized it," Whitney said. "Then watching it—some of my coworkers had clips, so I saw it. Watching the reruns when we were at NBC I was like, 'Wow, okay' and I realized how much they showed my mom and my sister and me."

Debbie Phelps also "cashed in" to a degree after the Olympics. Being a good mom paid off literally, as Johnson & Johnson named her "Mom of the Olympic Games," and did a commercial for her. The company whose clothes she wore, Chico's—a place where she's shopped for years—also brought her on-board as an endorser.

"She has a great eye for pulling things together, even with decorating," Hilary says. "She can pull something from here, and something from there, and always look good. She has loved shopping at Chico's for as long as I can remember, and can pull an outfit and awesome jewelry together in world-record time. Her style has evolved over the years, but she always looks great, don't you think?"

Whitney cautioned that her mom always dressed that way—that she was not just doing it for the endorsement deal because she had bought her clothes before NBC made her a household face and name at the 2008 Olympics.

"She always looks nice—she can't walk out the door without putting makeup on," Whitney said with a smile. "That's just how she is. Michael is her baby, that's her son, and she likes to look nice, no matter where she is. At this stage in my life I am happy to get out the door without baby food or formula on me. I have never been one to get all fru-fru with clothes and makeup."

Hilary remembers the period of time when her brother went from "being a swimmer" to showing signs of greatness.

"I remember when I was in college, and Michael was swimming at Senior Nationals," Hilary said. "I think he was thirteen or fourteen when he won Rookie of the Meet, and I thought that was pretty cool. I remember he just kept dropping time, and had a really fast 400 IM that meet. Then, when he came from sixth on the last wall at Trials in 2000 to make the team in the 200 fly, I thought, 'Wow.' He was fifteen, and the youngest male in sixty-eight years to make the Olympic team. Shortly after the 2000 Olympics, he broke the world record in the 200 fly, and I was so excited for him. I'm not sure that I can point to one specific time, because he kept improving by leaps and bounds."

Though Whitney never competed against her brother, she remembers when she came home from UNLV after her first semester and realizing he had hit a teen growth spurt.

"The first time I came home from college, [I] got off the plane and saw him; he had grown and his voice had dropped," Whitney says. "I remember looking up at him instead of down. I think that is when I realized that I would no longer be beating him and I also realized that he was no longer my 'little' brother."

While the Chinese culture and the sights they took in left Whitney with great memories, seeing her brother on the podium—on the top step—after every single one of his finals was what she'll never forget.

"The biggest things about China for me were Michael's performances," Whitney said. "Having him become the most decorated athlete ever and get eight gold medals. Michael does not get very emotional, and watching him take every moment in and seeing his eyes water made me thankful that we were able to go. I don't get to see that side of Michael very often."

Hilary is also touched and affected by the emotion she saw from her brother.

"It still has yet to really sink in, but I feel so very fortunate that we were there to see Michael and support him in his awesome achievements," Hilary says. "I was very emotional, because I know how hard he works, and the time that he puts into training, and it was great to see that it all really paid off for him. Seeing him on the platform, filled with happiness and sometimes overcome with emotion was really special for us. We're a pretty tight family unit."

Hilary says that not everyone gets to see her brother's sensitive side because he can be shy publicly, but that in all family matters he is thoughtful.

"He is very kind and incredibly caring," she says. "He always makes time for others in his busy schedule, and he has shown up unannounced several times to surprise my mom. One Mother's Day he wanted to come home and surprise Mom, and Whitney and I were in on it; we had done some fun things earlier that afternoon, and knew that we had to have Mom back to the house for the surprise. He could have just told her that he was coming in, but he's really thoughtful, and thought it would be more fun to surprise her. He had made reservations, and after the surprise, we all went out and laughed about it."

As a former swimmer, Hilary says that Michael really had a lot to overcome in the 200 fly, and that the 100 fly was as close as it gets.

"There were two that really stood out; [one was] the 200 fly, because to overcome the anxiety of having water fill your goggles is really tough. To hear that he counted strokes the last lap, was really impressive, and reminds me that if your heart and your mind are in it, you can overcome anything. The second was the 100 fly, because what a great finish. He took that extra half-stroke, which swimmers are taught not to do. But he knows himself so well, and instinctively took that last stroke, which won him the race. I remember looking at him as he got closer to the wall thinking, 'I hope he has a great finish.'"

Whitney almost didn't make the trip to China, however.

"My husband and I weren't going to go," Whitney says. "With the two kids and me taking maternity leave this year we had to figure out some arrangements. My husband's parents helped us out tremendously and took the kids for the twelve days that we were gone and my work was gracious to give me the time off."

While Whitney was a bit better known from her national experience as a swimmer, Hilary said even some of her coworkers did not make the connection that she and Michael were related.

"It's a little weird, because I have friends and work colleagues who had no idea," Hilary says. "I would say 'I'm going to Omaha [where the 2008 Olympic Trials were] to watch my brother swim.' After returning from China, they would say, 'I had no idea! Why didn't you tell me?' To me, I was watching my brother swim. And he just happens to be the greatest swimmer in the world, but it's odd now that everyone knows. But, on the other hand, it's cool that everyone knows who he is, because he's accomplished his goal of elevating the sport of swimming. When I overhear people in a restaurant talking about his accomplishments, it makes me smile."

One reason Whitney can relate to Michael so well is because she and Michael are so much alike.

"My mom and sister are extremely emotional," Whitney said. "Michael and I are alike, which can be good and can be bad, because we hold things in. I don't cry that much, but when I saw Michael tear up, it made me tear up. I don't see that side of him often. Being the same way, I knew that for him to get to that point that he was in the moment, enjoying it and proud of himself."

But Whitney realized part of the reason Michael could not show so much emotion after each medal is because he often had another race to swim in, usually a preliminary or semifinal, which he had to do well in to even advance to the final for each particular event.

"Sometimes he got off the medal stand and went right to a semifinal," Whitney says.

Hilary says Michael's focus was a key to his success in Beijing, and that Coach Bob Bowman's planning fits in well with that.

"Michael has the incredible ability to block out everyone and do what he and Bob have planned," Hilary says. "I was more worried going into Athens than I was headed into Beijing. I just want Michael to achieve his goals and do what he sets out to do. Seeing a look of disappointment on his face is really upsetting. I knew that he and Bob had a plan in place, as well as a strategy for execution. Michael has said that he didn't know what to expect heading into Athens, so this time around, he had a better idea of what was going on at the Games. Athens gave Michael experience."

Michael's Olympic career started in Sydney,

Australia, a place where swimming is as popular as football and baseball are in America. In 2004, Michael started on the path to become one of the best Olympians of all time in one of the world's most historic cities: Athens, Greece. Finally, Michael reached the pinnacle and carved his place in modern history in a country that has established itself as a force to be reckoned with, that can't be overlooked. His sisters are proud how much their brother has accomplished over the course of three Olympic Games in eight years. Hilary still remembers the moment at the 2000 Games in Sydney when Michael finished fifth to gold-medal winner Tom Malchow, the American from the University of Michigan who dominated the 200 butterfly before Michael took ownership of the event.

"I remember sitting with my mom in the stands and watching Michael come out onto the pool deck and tie his suit," Hilary said. "After that, he went over to Tom Malchow and shook his hand, wishing him luck. Michael looked nervous, and so young. We were able to spend some time with him after his race in Sydney, and he was smiling and happy. I had no idea at that time that it would mushroom into what it was in Beijing."

Chapter 22

From the Great Wall, to the Great Beyond

Since the Games started on August 8, 2008, at 8:08 local time in Beijing—and since Michael Phelps finished carrying the weight of eight gold medals, he said the run of eights continuing was pretty special.

"I guess it's a lucky number for me now, too," Phelps says. "Seeing 8-08 and the opening ceremony start at 8:08, I guess it was maybe meant to be. I don't know. For this to happen, everything had to fall into perfect place. If we had to do this again, I don't know if it would happen exactly the way we wanted it to, to the T."

The man who supplanted Mark Spitz, the winner of seven gold medals at the 1972 Munich Olympics, as the greatest swimmer in Olympic history couldn't have been happier with his results in Beijing. Prior to the start of the Games, Spitz said he viewed himself as the sporting equivalent as the first to walk on the moon. If Phelps got seven, Phelps would be the second to walk on the moon. If Phelps won eight gold medals, Spitz said, that would be like being the first to walk on Mars.

"First of all, records are always made to be broken, no matter what they are," Phelps says. "Anybody can do anything they set their mind to. I've said it all along: I want to be the first Michael Phelps, not the second Mark Spitz. Never once will I ever downplay his accomplishments, by any means. What he did still is an amazing feat and will always be an amazing accomplishment in the swimming world and also the Olympics. Being able to have something like that to shoot for, I think it made those days where you were tired, where you just wanted to go home and sleep, it made those days easier. To look at him and say 'I want to do this,' it's something that I've wanted to do and I'm thankful for having him do what he did."

Once he had finished with the relay, hugged his teammates, and picked up his eighth medal, Michael Phelps was about to have the chance to rest—but first, he had to talk, first of all, to his relay teammates. After they won on Lezak's final sprint, Phelps and the rest of the 400 medley relay swimmers—Brendan Hansen, Aaron Peirsol and Jason Lezak—had an extended group hug. Phelps said his teammates told him they were proud of him.

"They said congratulations," Phelps said. "We had a goal of winning all three relays, and we accomplished that goal, and I said to them, 'All this wouldn't be possible without the help' from them and other relay members. There was a lot of emotion in it, but that's what happens in sports."

His goals for the future are, not surprisingly, swimming related, a large part of which will be promoting the sport. After all, Phelps started swimming because his mother wanted him to be safe when they were around pools or at the beach. His hometown Baltimore Ravens broadcast his race live to fans during an exhibition game.

"From here, I guess I continue with my goal of raising the sport of swimming as high as I can in the United States," Phelps said. In referring to how the Olympics were covered in 2008, Phelps said that there were fans in "Raven Stadium watching the finals of the 400 relay tonight live, with seventy thousand people. People all over the place are saying it's crazy. They're going out to eat, the TV's on and swimming's on. I think the goal that I have and am working towards is in progress. I think it's going to take some time to get it where I want it."

The final relay was also shown at several other major sporting venues, including a Cincinnati Reds baseball game, and an announcement was made to cheers at Yankee Stadium—all this for the man who would soon head to Wall Street and stare at his pick of endorsement deals with corporate America.

While the financial windfall was about to start, Phelps pointed out before leaving Beijing that his swimming career wasn't a dash for cash.

"I'm not doing it for the money. I'm doing it because I love what I do. This is something I dreamed of as soon as I started swimming—winning an Olympic gold medal. In Athens I was able to do that. I was able to surpass my goals. If Bob and I were in it for the money, I think we'd be in different sports. It's definitely not about money. I'm having fun at what I do and I do this because I love it. That's really the only thing I can say. I enjoy it, and I couldn't ask for anything more. Every day it seems like I'm in sort of a dream world. Sometimes you sort of have to pinch yourself to see if it's really real. I'm just happy I'm in the real world, I guess."

Swimming is in a predicament as an Olympic sport because it only gets a lot of mainstream media attention every four years. Yet the World Championships are held every year that there is no Olympic Games, and the level at Worlds is the same at the Olympics.

"I don't want this sport to be an every-four-years sport," Phelps says. "Yes, we get the most attention every four years, but every year between those four, there's really not as much exposure for us as I would like. It has grown a lot over the last eight years, don't get me wrong. It has skyrocketed. But we swim every single day of the year. There's never really an off-season. I just want more people to get involved in the sport, be aware of what we're doing. And I really think it's going to happen. It's something that I'm proud and honored to be a part of, and honored to help the sport for the next generation of swimmers who come through here to have it better than we have it. This sport has changed my life and allowed me to do so many things. To have the younger generation experience more, I can't imagine what the sport is going to be like in ten years."

Phelps estimated he had been drug tested about 40 times leading up to, and through, the Olympics, something he said is "good for the sport." However, he was ready for a break—from everything, including the attention and swimming.

Many inside the swimming world knew who Phelps was before Athens. The likes of Natalie Coughlin and Dara Torres were also well-known. The China Games, however, brought the names and faces to the casual sports fan who tuned in to watch the Olympics, especially since swimming received so much television coverage from NBC during the daily telecasts, and dominated newspaper and cable television coverage around the world as well.

"I think it's really getting more of an awareness for the sport, for the U.S.," Phelps said. "It started four years ago and I think it's continued the last four years. So I think with the help from our team and this coaching staff, this sport can take off even more than it has. I think that's a goal that isn't going to happen overnight; it's going to happen over time. That's something I'm ready to do in the long haul."

While Phelps was understandably drained after all the preliminaries, semifinals and finals—as well as all the other energy that's expended at an event such as the Olympics, including the pressure to catch Spitz—he said he felt most taxed after the semifinals of the 100 fly. With two more events left, he knew he had to rest.

"After the semi of the 100 fly, I just absolutely said, 'Oh, my gosh'—it was a tough day, and one of the biggest reasons I was able to close out is because I was able to rest so much in-between, I had more down time," Phelps said. "Literally, I sat in my bed and watched movies or slept. One of the biggest things in why I was able to do this was being able to recover. Getting the ice baths, getting massages, eating and sleeping properly. It wasn't just the training that helped me do this."

While most fans, especially Americans, had their favorite moment—likely the 100 butterfly final, or the two relays in which teammates, notably Jason Lezak, delivered clutch performances—Phelps had all the individual moments to take home with him for the rest of his life.

Outside of the competition, the 2008 Games marked the first time that Phelps was finally "one of the guys" with the older swimmers, the ones who had or were wrapping up their college careers at the 2004 Olympics when Michael was still at North Baltimore and hadn't yet headed off to college.

While all week other swimmers were asked what they thought about Michael Phelps, the man who wears that name—and carries the eight medals with it—finally was asked about it.

"I'm lucky to have everything I have," Phelps said. "I'm lucky to have the talent that I have, the drive that I have, the excitement about the sport. I'm fortunate for every quality that I have, and I wouldn't trade any of it in."

In the pool, Phelps figures to once again change up his events. He surprised a lot of people in 2004 by adding the 200 meter freestyle, even though he'd have to go against world-record-holder Ian Thorpe. But that experience—Thorpe did win and Phelps narrowly missed placing second, instead settling for a bronze—shaped Phelps into what would become his march to dominate and own the world record in the 200 free.

Phelps was also potentially poised in 2004 to make the Olympic team in the 100 backstroke, and had beaten world-record holder and teammate Aaron Peirsol at a pre-Olympic Trials meet in the 100 back.

However, Phelps dropped that event, and it was probably for the better, because Peirsol is a team leader and veteran. Going after what was largely thought to be Peirsol's own event might have caused bad blood between Phelps and the "Texas trio" of Crocker, who was already his largest personal competitor nationally in the 100 fly, Brendan Hansen and Peirsol.

On the day he won his eighth medal in Beijing, Phelps said his program will be tweaked again. He admitted he and Bowman agreed that he would no longer have to keep the grueling 400 individual medley as part of his routine, and it seems like he will now go for a spot likely in the 100 backstroke whether Peirsol retires or not at this point, and perhaps even the 100 freestyle, though the 100 breaststroke is not out of the question just judging by how strong Phelps' breaststroke splits were in his IM events. Since Hansen's performance declined from 2004 to 2008, where he did not qualify for the U.S. team in the 200 breaststroke and did not medal at the Olympics in the 100 breaststroke, Phelps may add the breaststroke sprint as well. So Phelps' eye is on a new event or two, provided he drops at least one or two events from his current program, something he and Coach Bob Bowman will decide.

"I keep saying I want to go down and start sprinting, but Bob really isn't so keen on that—I don't think that's going to happen," Phelps said. "Over the next four years, I'd like to try some different events, maybe not do some of the events I did here. Bob has said that he wants to start fresh, do things that he hasn't done before. Try new things at workouts. Try new training methods. It's going to be a fun four years."

Appendix A:
Glossary of Terms

Active drag: The resistance caused by the actual stroke the athlete does. This is drag that can never go away entirely, but by increasing efficiency and making the body as hydrodynamic as possible, it can be reduced.

Drag: To drag off another athlete is to essentially surf on their wave. It is optimized generally when one athlete is at the hip of the athlete in the adjacent lane. Jason Lezak did this perfectly in the 400 freestyle relay when he "dragged" off of his French competitor who swam right next to his lane line, and Jason swam as close as he could get. It allowed Jason to conserve energy and finish the second half of the race extremely well.

Dry-land: Any exercise not in the pool. Includes weights, biking, running, sit-ups and the like.

Club (Age Group) Teams and Coaches: There is a distinction between the different kinds of teams that make up the landscape of swimming in the United States. "Club" teams are year-round swim teams that register the athletes with USA Swimming annually. They are sometimes called "Age Group" teams, as the kids are separated and compete against each other based on their ages. Many kids begin swimming on summer-league teams that only compete for the three months in the summer. There are also high school and college swimming teams and coaches, as well as YMCA.

IM, or Individual Medley: There are two individual medley races contested in the sport of swimming, the 200 and 400 IMs. They are a combination of all four legal strokes in this order: butterfly, backstroke, breaststroke and freestyle. In the 200, the athlete will complete 50 meters or one lap of each discipline, and for the 400, the athlete will complete 100 meters or two laps of each.

Lane Lines: The floating dividers between the lanes. The lane lines in international competition are usually "wave-eaters." This means that due to the design of the plastic, waves actually hit the lane lines and are diminished, making it more difficult to "drag" off the athlete in the adjacent lane.

Ready Room: The waiting or staging area the athletes must report to prior to the start of the final of their event at high-level competitions. The ready room is where the athletes are marshaled so they can all parade out together for the start of their race.

The "Tee": At the end of each lane six feet away from the wall, there is an image of a "T" laid into the tile on the bottom of the pool. Athletes routinely use this as a marker for them to time their turns effectively. That way, they don't have to crook their necks to spot the wall, but rather they can maintain their straight body line.

Underwater Dolphin Kicking: Athletes are allowed fifteen meters after a start or a turn to break the surface of the water. In the backstroke and butterfly especially, athletes take advantage of the full fifteen meters of space to streamline themselves and dolphin kick. This has been proven to be faster than the actual swimming if done well, so athletes like Michael Phelps and Ryan Lochte who do it well have an advantage.

Appendix B:
Strokes

There are four strokes in swimming: butterfly, back-stroke, breaststroke and freestyle.

Butterfly is an undulating stroke where the feet must remain together for the kick and the arms recover at the same time. The swimmer usually breathes forward.

Backstroke is done on the back, alternating arm strokes. Challenges in backstroke include going in a straight line (when you can't see where you're going, since you're on your back), and therefore hitting lane lines, and timing the underwater kick portion to come up at the fifteen meter mark (the distance limit legally allowed).

Breaststroke is also a somewhat undulating stroke, although not as fluid as the butterfly. The recovery is below the surface, and the kick is a "frog" kick.

Challenges in breaststroke mostly have to do with timing and limiting "active drag."

Freestyle is most recognizably the "crawl" stroke on the stomach where the arm strokes alternate. Freestyle can actually be any stroke at all, thus the name "freestyle." As long as the athlete touches the wall when he or she turns and finishes the required distance without pulling on the lane line or impeding another athlete's progress, the stroke is legal.

Appendix C:
Major Events on the
U.S. Swim Calendar

Olympics Games: Held every four years in various locations.

World Championships (Worlds): Held every other year (odd-numbered), so for example, 2001, 2003, 2005, 2007.

Pan-Pacific Games (Pan-Pacs): Held on even years, participants include swimmers from Australia, Asia, and North and South America.

Appendix D:
Author Interview

Why did you write this book?
Bob: I wanted to provide a couple of things. First of all, I wanted a keepsake for all fans, for everyone to remember what a great event the Olympics was, and a moment in history—Mark Spitz being an icon thirty-six years later is proof of how significant someone like this becomes as part of our pop culture. So I hope it has value as a collector's item to fans, and even as an unbiased record of what happened—though I was cheering as hard as anyone on the relays and especially the 100 fly. Secondly, I wanted to make sure a lot of the people who helped make Beijing 2008 happen for Michael were included in the telling of this story, people like relay teammates Jason Lezak, Ben Wildman-Tobriner, Aaron Peirsol, Brendan Hansen, Garrett Weber-Gale and others, including those who turned in record-setting performances in the preliminaries. Michael

did win five individual medals, but those relay teammates are what helped get him three more.

How did you write it?

Bob: I've done more than a hundred interviews with Olympic and World team swimmers, and wrote thousands of words about Michael, and tens of thousands more about the others, including his coach Bob Bowman, while I was a freelance writer contributing to "20 Question Tuesday" for USA Swimming's Web site. In fact, I saw these comments I first printed in news stories through the years since I started writing "20 Questions;" the USA Swimming Web site is used to promote the sport, so reporters are welcome to use the quotes from my stories there, and they do, at will. I saved those interviews, in which I often asked far more questions than I ever used for stories, a habit I developed as a journalist. I also used press conference transcripts for this book. When I use information from a news story in this book, I cite it at that moment, and I kept it to what I, as a former journalist, considered reputable newspapers—major metropolitan papers— and The Associated Press, and cited them all on every reference. I did not use the two previous books about Michael, and read neither. I had planned to; the one he wrote in 2004 did not "sound" like him to me when I read a brief excerpt on Google Books when I was thinking about ordering it. That book did not always, to me, at least, having interviewed Michael several times, capture his voice. So I focused on what I had done personally, and journalists who I knew would use quotes in ethical ways—without changing the words, or context. This actually started out as a pitch I wrote to write Michael's book. When they chose a former *L.A. Times* writer, I decided to write a book anyway. I was just calling his former teammates for special moments or stories, and a few of them told me about how he really hurt his hand or wrist. Then I realized there was some stuff he probably wouldn't want to talk about, so it worked out well that I was doing a separate book rather than his own.

What specifically is this book going to get attention for?
Bob: The book is going to get a lot of attention for just a few things—how he broke his hand in 2006, his sister's eating disorder, and a few other things. All totaled together, this book is 99-percent positive—it's more than 50,000 words, and not even 500 are what could be termed negative, so it's probably more than 99-percent positive. But it's also honest—it was more important to have a book with 100-percent integrity than be 100-percent glorification, though what he did is phenomenal. There's a nasty habit in print media these days to build up people to high by omitting certain facts—or not even asking certain questions. There's the opposite side of just

taking potshots in blogs and on message boards with no facts to back them up by "media comman-does" who have an agenda, or who are just plain mean. You need all the information, and to present it so people can get a full picture. I like Michael, im-mensely. He is good hearted and kind. But I don't know how a book with him working with him would have worked. He kept saying in interviews on NBC that he was "speechless," and while that's the perfect sound bite to lead into a commercial, it leaves print journalists scratching their heads, and unfortunately many fill in the blanks with how they think he felt. Michael is usually more reflective than insightful, and in general probably more thoughtful than articulate. He has a heart of gold and is one of the truly kind-hearted people in sports, but after writing first-person for more than 20 biographies, I knew he would be a tough one even if I would have gotten the chance to work with him, though he's such a nice person. That being said, he can talk swimming to no end, especially the technical as-pects, though I don't think that would have helped me had we worked together on a book.

Appendix E:
Phelps' Career Statistics

2000 Olympic Games
Sydney, Australia
Event/Results
200 butterfly/5th place

2001 World
   Championship
Fukuoka, Japan
Event/Results
200 butterfly/Gold Medal

2003 World
   Championships
Barcelona, Spain
Event/Results
100 butterfly/Silver Medal
200 butterfly/Gold Medal
200 individual medley/
   Gold Medal

400 individual medley/
   Gold Medal

2004 Olympic Games
Athens, Greece
Event/Results
400 individual
   medley/Gold Medal
100 butterfly/Gold Medal
200 freestyle/Bronze Medal
200 butterfly/Gold Medal
200 individual medley/
   Gold Medal
4 x 100 freestyle relay/
   Bronze Medal
4 x 200 freestyle relay/
   Gold Medal
4 x 100 medley relay/
   Gold Medal

**2005 World
Championships
Montreal, Canada
Event/Results**
200 individual
  medley/Gold Medal
400 freestyle relay/
  Gold Medal
200 freestyle/Gold Medal
800 freestyle relay/
  Gold Medal
100 fly/Silver Medal
400 medley relay/
  Gold Medal

**2007 World
Championships
Melbourne, Australia
Event/Results**
200 freestyle/Gold Medal
100 butterfly/Gold Medal
200 butterfly/Gold Medal
200 individual medley/
  Gold Medal
400 individual medley/
  Gold Medal

4 x 100 freestyle relay/
  Gold Medal
4 x 200 freestyle relay/
  Gold Medal
4 x 100 medley relay/
  Disqualified in
  preliminary heat

**2008 Olympics
Beijing, China
Event/Results**
400 individual medley/
  Gold Medal
4 x 100 freestyle relay/
  Gold Medal
200 freestyle/Gold Medal
200 butterfly/Gold Medal,
  World Record
4 x 200 freestyle relay/
  Gold Medal
200m individual medley/
  Gold Medal
100 butterfly/Gold Medal
4 x 100m medley relay/
  Gold Medal

Appendix F:
June 30: A Day that Brought the World Michael Phelps— and a Whole Lot More

Michael Phelps was born on June 30, 1985.

The day is special or memorable for a lot of people, going both way back in history and also on his more recent birthdays.

First of all, on Michael's birthday in 1985, thirty-nine American hostages who had spent seventeen days on an airplane hijacked in Beirut, Lebanon, were freed.

Michael also shares the day of June 30 as a birthday with former heavyweight boxing champion Mike Tyson, who was born in 1966. *American Idol* winner Fantasia Barrino was born on June 30, 1984, the year before Michael. Fantasia won *Idol* in 2004, the same year Michael won six gold medals and two bronze medals at the 2004 Athens Olympics.

The day in the course of history has also had its notable moments. On June 30, 1559, France's King Henry II was hurt in a jousting match.

Ironically, Michigan—where Michael swam from 2004 to 2008—was organized as a territory on June 30, 1805, by the U.S. Congress.

The big news event on June 30, 1859, was Charles Blondin, a French acrobat, crossing Niagara Falls—on a tightrope.

June 30, 1905, was a big day for science as Albert Einstein brought "special relativity" to the world with his article "On the Electrodynamics of Moving Bodies."

The Night of the Long Knives on June 30, 1934, was Adolph Hitler's horrid purge of political opponents and rivals in Germany.

June 30 also holds a pair of special memories for World War II for a competing reason, as on the date in 1941, Germany captured Lviv, Ukraine, and on June 30, 1944, the Battle of Cherbourg—part of the Battle of Normandy—concluded with a key port won by American forces.

Speaking of Michigan and things that move fast, the first Chevrolet Corvette was rolled off the assembly line in Michigan on June 30, 1953.

Three years later, in one of the most memorable domestic air tragedies of the era, two airliners, one from TWA and another from United Airlines, collided above the Grand Canyon, killing all people on both planes—one hundred twenty-eight total.

The day of June 30, 1997, was a big day for China as England transferred sovereignty of Hong Kong to the People's Republic of China.

The day in the course of history has also had its notable moments. On June 30, 1559, France's King Henry II was hurt in a jousting match.

Ironically, Michigan—where Michael swam from 2004 to 2008—was organized as a territory on June 30, 1805, by the U.S. Congress.

The big news event on June 30, 1859, was Charles Blondin, a French acrobat, crossing Niagara Falls—on a tightrope.

June 30, 1905, was a big day for science as Albert Einstein brought "special relativity" to the world with his article "On the Electrodynamics of Moving Bodies."

The Night of the Long Knives on June 30, 1934, was Adolph Hitler's horrid purge of political opponents and rivals in Germany.

June 30 also holds a pair of special memories for World War II for a competing reason, as on the date in 1941, Germany captured Lviv, Ukraine, and on June 30, 1944, the Battle of Cherbourg—part of the Battle of Normandy—concluded with a key port won by American forces.

Speaking of Michigan and things that move fast, the first Chevrolet Corvette was rolled off the assembly line in Michigan on June 30, 1953.

Three years later, in one of the most memorable domestic air tragedies of the era, two airliners, one from TWA and another from United Airlines, collided above the Grand Canyon, killing all people on both planes—one hundred twenty-eight total.

The day of June 30, 1997, was a big day for China as England transferred sovereignty of Hong Kong to the People's Republic of China.